BOSTON'S OLDEST BUILDINGS

AND WHERE TO FIND THEM

Joseph M. Bagley

# BOSTON'S

# Oldest Buildings

## and Where to Find Them

**UPDATED NEW EDITION**

Brandeis University Press | Waltham, Massachusetts

Brandeis University Press
© 2021 by Joseph M. Bagley
Foreword © 2025 by Robert J. Allison
All rights reserved
Manufactured in the United States of America
Designed by Mindy Basinger Hill
Typeset in Adobe Jenson Pro

For permission to reproduce any of the material in this book,
contact Brandeis University Press, 415 South Street, Waltham MA 02453,
or visit brandeisuniversitypress.com

Unless otherwise noted, all house photos are by the author.

Library of Congress Cataloging-in-Publication Data

Names: Bagley, Joseph M., 1985– author.
Title: Boston's oldest buildings and where to find them / Joseph M. Bagley.
Description: Waltham, Massachusetts : Brandeis University Press, [2021] |
    Includes bibliographical references and index. | Summary: "A guidebook
    for Boston's 50 oldest buildings. Written in a conversational manner
    that does not bog the reader down in technical jargon, but allows them
    to see the history of Boston through the lens of its oldest structures
    while appreciating decades of efforts to preserve its built
    environment" —Provided by publisher.
Identifiers: LCCN 2020054073 (print) | LCCN 2020054074 (ebook)
    ISBN 9781684580392 (paperback) | ISBN 9781684580408 (ebook)
Subjects: LCSH: Historic buildings—Massachusetts—Boston—Guidebooks.
    Historic buildings—Massachusetts—Boston—Pictorial works.
    Historic buildings—Conservation and restoration—Massachusetts—Boston.
    Historic preservation—Massachusetts—Boston.
    Boston (Mass.) —Buildings, structures, etc. —Guidebooks.
    Boston (Mass.) —Buildings, structures, etc. —Pictorial works.
    Boston (Mass.) —History—Pictorial works. | Boston (Mass.) —Guidebooks.
    Repeat photography—Massachusetts—Boston.
Classification: LCC F73.37 .B325 2021 (print) | LCC F73.37 (ebook)
    DDC 974.4/61—dc23
LC record available at https://lccn.loc.gov/2020054073
LC ebook record available at https://lccn.loc.gov/2020054074

5  4  3  2

COVER ILLUSTRATIONS Figure 2.2 courtesy of Paul Revere Memorial
Association; Figures 7.1, 35 Main, 6.2, 16 Main, 8.1, 26 Main, 28.1, and 40 Main
are works by the author or are in public domain.

THIS BOOK IS DEDICATED

TO THE BOSTON PRESERVATION COMMUNITY.

Take away these expressions of the soul,

of the life of Boston, and what, I ask,

have you left beyond any other city on the continent?

REV. WILLIAM H. H. MURRAY | quoted in Edward Watson Burdett, *History of the Old South Meeting-House in Boston*

# Contents

# Foreword

Robert J. Allison, Suffolk University

If you are reading this book, you likely are already among the converted. You value and want to preserve older buildings that tell stories. Please share the book with those who are indifferent, or those outright against preserving these and other witnesses to history.

Boston's historic fabric, represented here by a small sampling of its earliest buildings, is always under threat, but most particularly when the very things that make it an attractive place, such as its historic landscape which has nurtured so many innovations and innovators, attracts more people who need places to live and work. In building a new Boston, which we have been doing continually since 1630, we have often simply obliterated the old. As this book tells us, these surviving buildings allow us to know where we have been. Through them we can know some of the many stories of Boston.

As a new Boston was being built in the 1960s on the razed site of Scollay Square, a Boston city councilor is purported to have said that when people come to Boston they want to see shiny new revenue-generating buildings, like those they would see in Houston or Miami; they did not want to see the crummy old printing shop where William Lloyd Garrison turned out *The Liberator*. The point of the anecdote is not that once upon a time a short-sighted imbecile was elected to public office in Boston, but rather that generally we have very good reasons to knock down an old building and replace it with a new one. It is in the city's interest to do so (I am not sure that visitors to Boston care how much revenue our buildings generate). Those of us reading the book, and already conscious of the value of these old buildings, need to do a better job of showing how it is in the city's interest to keep the older buildings, partly, as it turns out, because people do come here to see pieces of history that they cannot see anywhere else.

The venerable edifices surviving along Boston's Freedom Trail are here—the Paul Revere House, the nation's oldest urban dwelling; Old North Church and Old South Meeting House; Faneuil Hall; the Corner Book Store (tastes change: it now sells burritos rather than books). Fifteen of the fifty buildings you will learn about in this book are in the North End (the country's oldest neighborhood) or downtown. Some of them are well-known, though all have been threatened over the years by fire, demolition, or neglect.

But more notably, you will see historic buildings in other parts of Boston. Twelve of these historic buildings are in Dorchester, including the seventeenth-century James Blake House, the oldest house in the city. Three are in Roxbury, including the elegant Shirley-Eustis House, the elegant country estate Governor William Shirley built in the 1740s, and the eighteenth-century Dillaway-Thomas House, parsonage to Roxbury's First Church, and General John Thomas's headquarters during the Siege of Boston. Remarkably, since the entire town burned on June 17, 1775, nine buildings are in Charlestown. Two are in Mattapan, including the farmhouse Samuel Fowler built in 1786, and three are in Brighton.

Just off Faneuil Street in Brighton is a small non-descript house with a gambrel roof. This is all that remains of the 70-acre estate of Benjamin Faneuil, one of the wealthiest men in the British North America when he began amassing his property in the 1760s. He built an ostentatious mansion on the hill that rises beyond the small house, where his gatekeeper lived. On a July day in 1775 the gatekeeper—possibly a manservant enslaved by Faneuil's daughter Mary—came out of this house when he saw two distinguished military men ride past. He knew who they were. Generals George Washington and Charles Lee had just arrived in Cambridge to take command of the Continental Army. The gate keeper invited them to dine with the Faneuils. A smart move, as it might have prevented the house from being seized as Tory property. The reprieve was temporary, as an expanding town needed land (twentieth-century triple-deckers and apartments stand across the intersection), and the mansion itself burned in 1917. The gatekeeper's house is all that remains.

We might pass this house a hundred times and never see it. Hundreds of people, visitors and city residents, walk past 350 Hanover Street every day. Unless they are visiting the men's salon or the restaurant on the first floor, or renting an apartment upstairs, why would anyone take notice? It was not on Bagley's list when he began this project. But in photographing another building, he noticed the brick work on this one. Records suggested the house was built about 1814, but that did not seem right. He dug in to do more research. John Grant bought the property in 1734, probably built the house in 1735, and one of these houses—either the one he knocked down or the one he built—quite possibly is where Paul Revere was born. More remarkably, in 1795 sailmaker Levi Lane bought the property, sold it three years later to a sailor named William Ward, whose family lived there into the twentieth-century. This is Hanover Street's oldest surviving building.

Buildings have histories. But they need people to give them life and tell their stories. What buildings do we pass every day without a second or even first look? Who built these places? Why did they live here? What stories took shape here? These fifty buildings are a great start. There are many more. Among his Honorable Mentions, Bagley mentions some worthy structures that might be designated Landmarks, and some which are, such as the USS *Constitution*. Is the oldest commissioned warship still afloat in the world, the nation's official "ship of state," in need of protection like an old gate house in Brighton or a print shop in Scollay Square? The Navy thought of scrapping the obsolete vessel in the 1820s, stopped only by a Boston doctor's poetic plea to save her, and in the first decade of the twentieth-century Secretary of the Navy Charles Joseph Bonaparte thought the old ship's best use would be as a target for practicing the Navy's newer guns. Fortunately President Theodore Roosevelt not only understood history (simultaneously he was President of the United States, and of the American Historical Association), he cared about it.

Caring about it is the first and most important step to save any building. Buildings do not build themselves; they cannot tell their own stories; and they cannot save themselves. We owe thanks to the Boston Landmarks Commission, and to the yeoman work of the Boston Preservation Alliance, and Historic Boston, Inc., that so many of these structures remain. Bagley explains the process by which the Boston Landmarks Commission may designate a Landmark, for its architectural or historical significance. But the most critical part is to have people care enough to want to save one of these venerable witnesses to Boston's history.

It is hard to imagine Bostonians in two hundred years caring much about the boxes with windows being built around the city today. The builders of the gambrel-roofed carriage house in Brighton, of the Grant house on Hanover Street, the timber-framed Pierce and Blake houses, the brick row houses on Oak Street and Johnny Court in Chinatown, the brick Hawes House in South Boston or the Donald McKay house in East Boston, the triple-deckers and Greek-revival attached single-families throughout the city, were doing the same thing today's builders of undistinguished and forgettable structures are doing—building places in which to live and work. Why does the work of the earlier craftsmen endure so well?

But the bland boxes will be all that remain unless we care more about the historic buildings around us. Joseph Bagley is not hectoring the reader (as I am doing) but showing us how to care for these places that shape Boston. Thanks to Joseph Bagley for introducing us to these buildings, which can tell so many stories of Boston's past. It is now up to each of us to make sure these places and the stories they can tell are part of Boston's future.

# Preface

After my first book, *A History of Boston in 50 Artifacts*, I had the daft idea of writing a companion book on the fifty oldest buildings in Boston. It seemed like a great idea at the time, but when I began researching the construction dates of a few of the less-well documented buildings in this text, I quickly understood just how difficult this process was and why no one had done it before.

I am an archaeologist, and thus much of my research ahead of digs is focused on establishing the chronological history of a property from the time it was first built to the present. My goal in archaeology is to tell an interesting story, not just list every artifact found. That is the goal of this book, too, so I will try to stay clear of too much architectural description and jargon. As this book is not written for architectural historians, I hope that is to everyone's collective benefit.

While every effort was made to establish when these buildings were first built, it was always not possible to determine exact dates of construction through deeds, probates, or other available data. Less than 15 percent of the buildings in Boston have been surveyed for the Massachusetts Historical Commissions historic building inventory. There are 16,319 inventoried Boston buildings, or just 13.5 percent of the more than 121,000 buildings documented in the city. Though these individual survey forms can be extensive, some of Boston's most hidden old buildings may have been missed. There are other buildings whose estimated and reported construction dates placed them outside of the research scope of this book, but they may actually be older or younger than they have been reported to be. It is very possible that this list of Boston's oldest buildings will be refined over time with new data, but I did my best.

AUTHORS NOTE TO NEW EDITION 2024
Since the first publication of this book, additional research has revealed multiple buildings in Boston not originally included in this book to be some of Boston's oldest. I'm pleased to add 22-24 Shirley Street (ca. 1750) and the John Capen House (ca. 1781) to this edition of *Boston's Oldest Buildings*. They can be found added to the Honorable Mentions section of the book. I look forward to what else we discover while studying Boston's historical places.

# Acknowledgments

Many people and organizations have been instrumental in the creation of this book. First and foremost, my appreciation goes to the many researchers who came before me and whose work is cited throughout. The research in this book was greatly aided by digitized data provided by ancestry.com, ATLASCOPE, Boston City Archives, Boston Public Library, Dorchester Athenaeum, familysearch.org, Google Books, Historic Boston Incorporated, Historic New England, Leventhal Map Center, MACRIS, and mapjunction. com. The following individuals have directly contributed to the new research presented here: Tonya Loveday, Britton Mallard, Amy Ohman, Jake Rooney, and Kathleen von Jena. Lorie Komlyn, Jennifer Reed, and Jean Woy read early versions of this book and provided extensive and valuable comments and edits. Local historical groups were key in data gathering and building identification, but a special thank you to Julie Hall, Andrew Hatcher, Earl Taylor, and Amanda Zettel for their help in identifying buildings for this book. I am grateful for the assistance of many fact-checkers, including Marcia Butman, Dorothy Clark, Frederic Detwiller, Kent Edwards, Gretchen Grozier, Kathy Kottaridis, Bill Lamb, Patrick Leehey, Catherine Matthews, Judy McDonough, Amy Ohman, Byron Rushing, Robert Shimp, Gracelaw Simmons, Edith Steblecki, Earl Taylor, Charlie Vasiliades, Kathleen von Jena, Nina Zannieri, Amanda Zettel, the Jamaica Plain Historical Society, and the team at Old North Church and Historic Site. My gratitude and appreciation go to the amazing team at Brandeis University Press for publishing this work and for their enthusiasm and encouragement throughout the process. Finally, my appreciation and gratitude go to my amazing colleagues at the Boston Landmarks Commission, especially Executive Director, Rosanne Foley, who allowed this book to happen.

# BOSTON'S OLDEST BUILDINGS

# AND WHERE TO FIND THEM

# Introduction

It was the ideas in the minds of Bostonians that attracted the wrath of England's King George III and founded a nation. It is here that historic buildings remain as silent witnesses of Boston's past. And it is here that history is respected.

This book celebrates the fifty oldest buildings in Boston and the stories they reveal. Each chapter features a building, listed in ranked order by age, and presents the story of when and why it was built, the interesting events and people associated with it, and the efforts that have gone into its preservation By the end of the book, you will have traveled to most of the neighborhoods of Boston; seen a wide variety of historic preservation efforts; and, I hope, learned a few interesting things about the place we call Boston. You will see the good, the bad, and the vinyl clad, but each of these buildings has a story.

These stories are under threat. With an ever-growing city comes the need to build housing, businesses, and other resources for residents. Some of the buildings in this book are heavily protected by organizations, laws, landmark status, and residents who support their continued existence and maintenance. Others have no protections, and you may have never heard of them.

Historic preservation is an ongoing and evolving endeavor. It takes a community of hard-working historic preservationists—including architectural historians, skilled craftspeople, local communities, archaeologists, architects, contractors, nonprofit organizations, and government employees—to protect significant buildings as a city grows and changes. These fifty buildings represent only 0.04 percent of the 121,000 buildings in Boston.[1] Can all of the buildings in this book be saved?

## EARLY HISTORIC PRESERVATION IN BOSTON

It was the early loss of buildings in Boston that ignited one of the first sparks of the US preservation movement. Throughout the nineteenth century, the city's growth required the construction of new and larger buildings, often at the expense of historic buildings. Multiple seventeenth-century structures, including the Old Feather Store (figure 1.1). In the North End, seventeenth-century houses, including one associated with Cotton Mather (figure 1.2), were replaced with apartment buildings. On Beacon Hill, a rapidly developing group of brick row houses sprawled outward, eventually arriving at the door of Hancock Manor.

In 1735, the merchant Thomas Hancock paid for the construction of a massive stone mansion on Beacon Hill facing Boston Common (figure I.3).[2] Thomas lived there with his wife, Lydia; their nephew, John Hancock, whom they had adopted; and their enslaved people, named Cato, Agnes, Violet, and Hannibal.[3] Thomas died in 1762, leaving his estate to John and Lydia. They remained in the house with their enslaved people until they were forced to flee during the Revolution.[4]

John and his new wife, Dorothy Quincy, reoccupied the house in 1777. Hancock was said to have given his house to the Commonwealth on his deathbed in 1793, but his will was never signed.[5] Ebenezer Hancock (see building #27), John's younger brother, therefore inherited the house and offered to sell it to the state for a governor's mansion, but the sale fell through. In 1863, the house was sold at auction to two local merchants, who offered the house to the state for free, so long as it was moved.[6] This effort also failed, and the house was slated for demolition.

In response, local residents published a broadside on June 6, 1863 (figure I.4), pleading both the residents of Boston and the owners of the building to halt the demolition. Ultimately unsuccessful, the outrage over the demolition of Hancock Manor in 1863 sparked the preservation movement in New England.

Several architectural elements of the house were saved and now reside in various museums, institutions, and parks. Just before the house's demolition,

FIGURE I.3
Drawing of
Hancock Manor
on Beacon Hill
around 1835
(BPL 1835; image
courtesy of
the BPL).

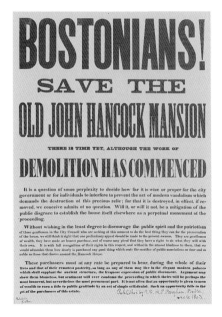

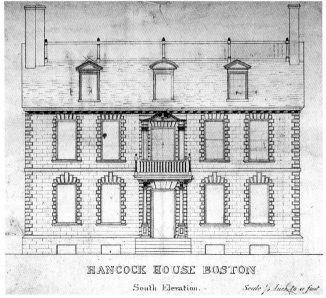

HANCOCK HOUSE BOSTON

South Elevation. Scale 1/8 inch to a foot

the architect John Hubbard Sturgis created seven scaled drawings of its interior and exterior, the first full set of measured drawings ever made of a house in America (figure 1.5).[7]

The fledgling preservation movement was soon tested again. In 1874, the congregation of Old South Meeting House (see building #16) decided to move to a new church in Back Bay. Despite an outcry, the building was sold for scrap at auction in June 1876, with sixty days to complete the demolition.[8] A clothing merchant and his son stepped in, buying the rights to stop the demolition for seven days—during which impassioned pleas were made by famous speakers in front of large crowds at the building to raise the $420,000 necessary to buy it.[9]

After securing another two-month delay to raise funds, a group of twenty wealthy Boston women joined together to form the Old South Association, which eventually raised or borrowed enough money to purchase the building and the land under in it in October 1876.[10] It was the first historic building to be saved in New England.

FIGURE 1.4 *left* 1863 broadside begging Bostonians to save the Hancock Manor (Sartan 1863; image courtesy of Historic New England [HNE]).

FIGURE 1.5 *right* Scaled drawing of the front facade of Hancock Manor (Sturgis 1863; image courtesy of HNE).

## EARLY HISTORIC PRESERVATION LAWS

Preservation awareness grew throughout the late nineteenth and early twentieth centuries. At the national level, the creation of the National Park Service's Historic American Buildings Survey (HABS) in 1933 sought to put out-of-work photographers, architects, and draftspeople to work during the Great

Depression. Teams of these people documented the nation's historic buildings through scaled drawings and images, and HABS documentation of historic buildings (both threatened and unthreatened) continues today.

As predominantly white populations moved out of cities in the mid-twentieth century, the Housing Act of 1949 and the Federal Aid Highway Act of 1956 created a push to demolish older buildings and so-called slums, build new structures and highways, and attract new residents and businesses to downtown areas in what was known as urban renewal. This led to the large-scale demolition of nearly one-third of the heart of Boston, including large portions of the West End, South End, Downtown, and Charlestown neighborhoods.

In response, Boston residents formed neighborhood organizations, including the West End Historical Association and the Charlestown Preservation Society, to fight to protect long-established communities and historic buildings. Wealthier, whiter, and less-threatened neighborhoods with more political power were able to successfully lobby the state to create the Historic Beacon Hill District (now called the Beacon Hill Architectural District) in 1955, the first legally defined historic district in Massachusetts. The regulations associated with the historic district required a commission to review proposed changes to historic buildings. The Back Bay Architectural District was established in 1966, creating the city's second heavily regulated and protected architectural area.

## FEDERAL AND STATE PROTECTIONS

Public outcry over the loss of historic buildings across the United States resulted in the National Historic Preservation Act of 1966. Section 106 of this legislation requires the review of projects that involve federal licensing, permitting, or funding to determine if they would have negative impacts on historic buildings and places and to determine whether the historic resource is or could be listed on the newly created National Register of Historic Places (National Register). The law also required mitigation if properties already on or eligible to be on the National Register were at risk due to federally funded projects. This law has created most of the historic preservation jobs in the United States. Massachusetts took these laws one step further, expanding their scope to include not just federal projects, but those funded, licensed, or permitted by the state as well. The Massachusetts Historical Commission (MHC) reviews these state and federal projects, but many changes to historic resources that do not require extensive permitting or funding are not reviewed. The strongest protections for historic properties can be found at the municipal level.

## THE BOSTON LANDMARKS COMMISSION

Beginning in the mid-1940s, more than seventy cities created landmarks commissions, including Philadelphia (in 1955), Baltimore (1964), and New York City (1965). These commissions allowed municipalities to give landmark status to areas and buildings and to require changes to them to be reviewed by a commission of local people. Though Back Bay and Beacon Hill were protected, Boston took longer than other cities to create a landmarks commission.

A 1974 *Boston Globe* opinion piece stated: "Part of the problem seems to be that no one realizes there IS a problem. Because Boston happens to be lucky enough to have a lot of good old buildings still around, many people assume that someone must be keeping an eye on them. Well, no one is."[11] In 1975, the architect Leslie Larson formed the City Conservation League to fight the demolition of the 1860s Jordan Marsh building in downtown Boston. Though unsuccessful in saving the building, the group's activism added momentum to the ongoing efforts to create a landmark commission in Boston.[12] The Boston Landmarks Commission (BLC) was finally created later in 1975.

Today, there are nine Landmark Districts and Conservation Areas in the city, in addition to over ninety individual properties designated as Landmarks. Over eight thousand Boston buildings, other structures, boats, parks, cemeteries, landscapes, and archaeological sites have that designation.

To be eligible for the designation, a historic resource must be deemed significant at the state or national level according to at least one of four criteria: it is listed on the National Register, associated with an important event, associated with an important individual, or an important contribution to architecture or landscape design. Because Landmark status provides the best levels of oversight and protection for historic resources across Boston, this book will indicate the Landmark status of each of the fifty buildings discussed here.

Achieving Landmark status for a historic resource begins with a petition signed by Bostonians. If the BLC accepts the petition as valid, resource becomes a pending Landmark while a Study Report is prepared. These reports include detailed historical research on the ownership and history of the resource, a detailed architectural description of it, and a discussion of its significance. The report concludes with a section titled "Standards and Criteria," an itemized list of the individual features of the building that must be conserved or enhanced to maintain its Landmark status. The report is the document used to review all future changes to the resource. If the Commissioners accept the report and vote to designate the resource a Landmark, and if both the mayor and city council approve, the property becomes a Boston Landmark.

Almost all changes to a Landmark are reviewed by BLC staff members. They make their recommendations to the Commissioners, who have the final vote on the changes.

## ARTICLE 85 (DEMOLITION DELAY)

In 1995, Article 85 of Boston's zoning code became law. Article 85 creates a demolition delay that requires that buildings at least fifty years of age be reviewed by the BLC before they are demolished. Once an application is received from the owner of the property wishing to conduct the demolition, BLC staff members have ten days to determine if the building could be significant or be a structure that, if lost, would create a significant and negative impact on the historical integrity of the neighborhood.

If the BLC staff determines that the building is not significant, the building can be torn down. But if the building is held to be significant, the applicant is required to hold a public community meeting and present alternatives to the demolition of the building. Afterward, the BLC staff schedules an official public hearing, at which the Commission members must decide if they agree that the building is significant and whether they will issue a ninety-day demolition delay for the building. In theory, the ninety days allows the applicant to apply the alternatives to demolition discussed in public community meetings and/or for the Landmark designation process to take place. Since the determination of eligibility for Landmark status requires proof that a building is significant at the state or national level, it is often not possible to award that status to a building threatened with demolition. In these situations, the hope is that the alternative plans will be enacted, saving the historic resource. However, if the property is not eligible to become a landmark, it can be demolished after ninety days. Fortunately, the BLC is not alone in the local fight to save historic properties in Boston.

## BOSTON PRESERVATION ORGANIZATIONS

Laws and regulations can go only so far to protect historic buildings and other resources in Boston. This book will celebrate the work of many organizations that own buildings included here and maintain them with significant effort and expense. At the city level, Historic Boston Incorporated (HBI), which appears multiple times in this work, stepped in at points of critical need to preserve historic places in Boston. Through its business savvy, preservation expertise, and community organization skills, it finds new and innovative ways not only to save and restore historic properties, but also to find meaningful adaptive reuse opportunities for historic places that bring vibrancy and new life to those places in need.

The Boston Preservation Alliance is particularly visible whenever a historic property is threatened. The organization's tireless efforts to make the public aware of threats, its ability to work directly with developers in an independent manner, and its vocal opposition to projects that threaten historic places ensure that threats to historic resources remain in the public eye.

Community-based organizations and individual residents may be the most important advocates for historic preservation, as there is no justification or broader support for political or legal actions without community support. These historical and preservation organizations have spent decades fighting to save the historic places in their neighborhoods and remain the strongest, most passionate, and most effective means of historic preservation in Boston.

As a city employee, I am forbidden from accepting outside payment for work as a staff member of the BLC. Therefore, all of the author's advance, proceeds, and royalties from the sale of this book will be transferred to the BLC to support its ongoing education, outreach, and historic preservation efforts in the city. It is my hope that the spotlight shone upon the properties in this book, coupled with the amplification provided by the agencies, groups, and individuals listed above, will ensure that these fifty buildings will never see the wrecking ball.

## BOSTON LANDMARK STATUS, NATIONAL REGISTER LISTING, AND NATIONAL HISTORIC LANDMARK STATUS: THE DIFFERENCES

This book will focus on designation as a Boston Landmark since this is the designation with the greatest ability to preserve historic buildings in the city. Many of the buildings in the book are not designated by the city as Landmarks, but some are National Historic Landmarks and listed on the National Register. So what's the difference?

Places listed on the National Register must be historically significant at the local, state, or national level. National Historic Landmarks are properties on the National Register that have national significance. Boston Landmarks must have "above local" significance, meaning significance at the state or national level. This means that a place may be locally significant and listed on the National Register but not qualify to be a Boston Landmark.

In Boston, changes to properties that are on the National Register or have National Historic Landmark status but are not Boston Landmarks are not reviewed by anyone unless the changes involve federal or state licenses, permits, or funding. Because almost all exterior changes to Boston Landmarks require review and approval of by the BLC, the protections of Boston Landmark status greatly exceed those of National Historic Landmark designation or of being listed on the National Register.

### BOSTON'S OLDEST BUILDINGS: THE GROUND RULES

As this book is fundamentally arranged in chronological order, a great deal of effort has gone into producing the most informed dating so far of the fifty buildings listed. Ground rules were necessary to contain the scope of the research needed to establish which buildings to include in this book: A Boston building must be structure with a roof and walls within the current legal boundaries of the City of Boston at the time of publication. It must be currently visible, have building elements above the foundation, be on land, be intended to house or be used by living humans, be originally designed to have both a roof and walls, and have historic elements that are arranged in rough approximation of its original form. The Honorable Mentions include buildings that were disqualified from inclusion because of these ground rules.

A building's age is determined from its oldest portions above the foundation that are visible from the exterior of the building. As you will see, this can include partial walls. Given that many wooden buildings in this book have had their exterior elements replaced, covered, or otherwise altered, this book includes wooden buildings whose exterior cladding has been heavily altered, replaced, or modified—which is somewhat unavoidable over centuries. The exact year of construction is known for only a few of the buildings in this book. Therefore, this text uses the following hierarchy of dating techniques to establish building dates: written records stating that the construction of a building has commenced; dendrochronology, which uses the outermost tree ring on a framing timber of a historic house to establish the latest season that a tree could have been standing before being felled and used in a home; deeds, which tend to indicate the presence or absence of a house and thus provide bookend dates for the existence of vacant land and that of a built structure; and architectural style, which is the least reliable dating option, as the personal taste of the builder or owner can dictate the use of a style before or after its period of popularity.

This book is fundamentally not about the structures themselves. It is not about quoins and muntins and the oldest or biggest. It is about the story of these places and the people associated with them. It is about Bostonians: the masons, glaziers, carpenters, laborers, housewrights, and many others who built these buildings; the many hundreds of people who were born, lived, and died in them; and the many who have worked in the past and present to ensure they stand today. It is about the life and soul of this city, and what makes Boston, Boston.

# Boston's Oldest Buildings

N

BRIGHTON / ALLSTON

MISSI
H

JAMAICA PLAIN

ROSLINDALE

WEST ROXBURY

HYDE PARK

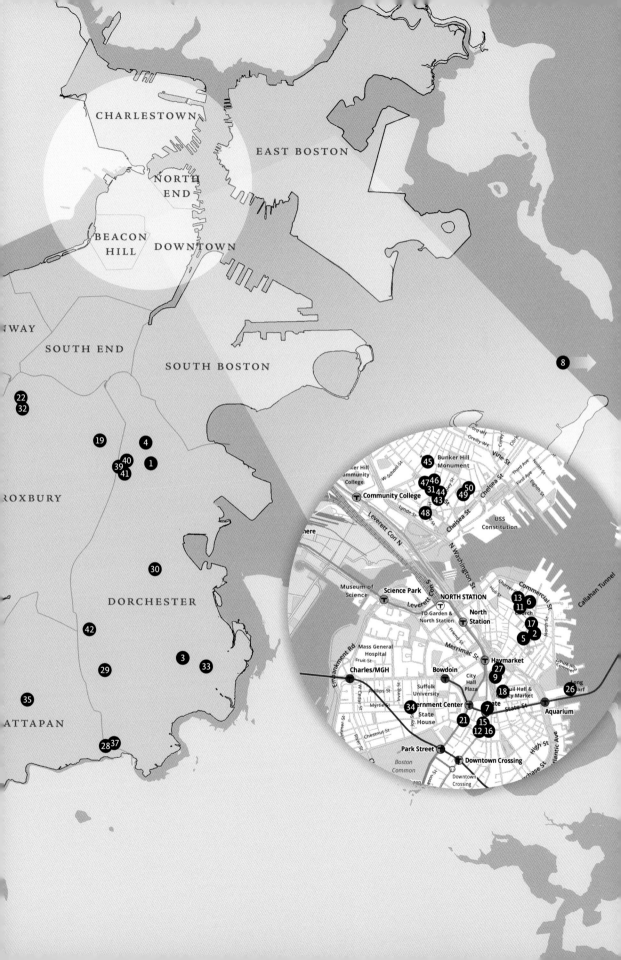

CHARLESTOWN

EAST BOSTON

NORTH
END

BEACON
HILL

DOWNTOWN

SOUTH END

SOUTH BOSTON

NWAY

ROXBURY

DORCHESTER

ATTAPAN

8

22
32

19

4

40
39 41

1

30

42

3

33

29

35

28 37

Bunker Hill
Monument

45

47 46
31 44
43

50
49

48

Community College

Chelsea St

USS
Constitution

Leverett Con N

Museum of
Science

Science Park

NORTH STATION

Commercial St

13
11

6

North
Station

Church

TD Garden &
North Station

17
5

2

Embankment Rd

Mass General
Hospital
Fruit St

Charles/MGH

Merrimac St

Haymarket

27
9

Bowdoin

City
Hall
Plaza

18

Faneuil Hall &
Quincy Market

26

Suffolk
University

Government Center

7

State St

Aquarium

34

State
House

21

15
12 16

Park Street

Downtown Crossing

Boston
Common

Downtown
Crossing

High St

Atlantic Ave

# 1. Blake House

735 Columbia Road, Dorchester | 1661

The James Blake House is Boston's oldest building. It stands within Richardson Park in the northern end of Dorchester. Long before it arrived at this location, the Blake House sat on a ten-acre parcel of farmland a few hundred feet to the northwest. This original site is now the parking lot of an Eversource building, just west of the South Bay shopping center.

The house was built in 1661 for James Blake and his wife, Elizabeth Clap, and it would remain in the Blake family until 1825.[1] Its interior (32 by 20 feet, or around 1,200 square feet over two stories) was quite large for its time. Most early houses in Massachusetts were built in an "East Anglia" style, named after the area northeast of London, where there were fewer trees and the

FIGURE I.1
Digitally reconstructed view of the Blake House showing the original front dormers and the larger diamond-pane casement windows that may also have once been on the building (photo and edits by author).

FIGURE I.2
The Blake House around 1890, just prior to its move. Note the double-hung windows and additions on either side of the main house, both of which were removed in the 1895 restoration (BPL 1890; image courtesy of the BPL).

architects learned to use less wood and smaller timbers in the framing of homes. Because the timbers in the house are large and numerous, architectural historians believe that the housewrights who built the Blake House were from the southwest corner of England, where trees were far more prevalent.[2] The Blake House is the older of two surviving houses in this building style in Massachusetts, the other being the ca. 1678 Coffin House in Newbury.

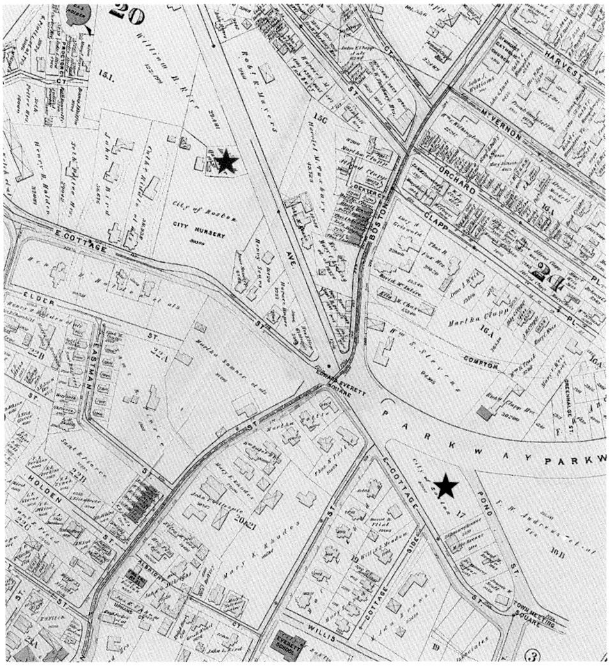

The original house had prominent front dormers, the outlines of which survive in the framing of the roof (figure 1.1). These would have provided additional living space in the attic.

In the eighteenth century, the Blake family removed the dormers, added additions to both sides of the house, and replaced the original three-sash casement windows with double-hung windows (figure 1.2).[3] Despite these changes to the exterior of the house, the interior retained many of its original elements, including doors and hinges.

The City of Boston purchased the house in 1895 to build greenhouses on the site.[4] The Dorchester Historical Society (DHS) sought the preservation of the building and received permission from the City of Boston to move the Blake House to Richardson Park for the society to use as a museum.[5]

Dorchester's seventeenth-century town common, a small pond, and the former 1630s First Church had been located at the eastern end of Richardson Park, making it an appropriate seventeenth-century landscape in which to place one of Boston's few remaining buildings from that century. Movers moved the house, excluding its later additions, in the winter of 1895, marking the first time a house was moved in New England for historic preservation (figure 1.3).[6]

The timing of this move was carefully planned. Conditions in winter would have frozen the ground, making it more durable during the move of the building, with its considerable weight. Once the house was lifted off its foundation, a sled-like structure would have been built under the building, and the house would have been lowered onto the sled and pulled by oxen or horses down the street on log rollers.

FIGURE 1.3 Map in an 1894 atlas published by G. W. Bromley and Company showing the location of the Blake House (the red star in the upper left) prior to its move and its location (the black star in the lower right) after its 1895 move (image courtesy of the Norman B. Leventhal Map Center; edits by author).

Standing in front of the house today at the intersection of Pond and Cottage Streets, you can imagine the house traveling down the street from Massachusetts Avenue, taking the slight bend at Pond Street, and being slowly maneuvered into its new home with the help of draught animals and watched by Dorchester residents.

Once the Blake House had arrived in its new site, it underwent a full restoration to what was believed to be an accurate representation of how it would have looked in the mid-seventeenth century, but there were some errors. For example, the 1895 team put back the diamond-pane casement windows, but they are likely smaller than the originals. The team also used multicolored Dutch glass, but the original windows would have been a consistent pale olive green.[7] Since this was one of the oldest house restorations of note in Boston, these changes have become part of the historic significance of the house and a notable part of the early historic preservation efforts.

The DHS received a state grant in 2007 for another restoration and chose to restore the Blake House to its 1895 appearance, because the restorations could be accurately guided by numerous photographs of the house from multiple angles after its move to the park.[8] This restoration also included dendrochronology, which used tree rings in a beam in the house to prove that the tree used in the house was cut in 1661.[9] The restoration team repaired the windows, removed the heavy slate roof, and added new cedar shingles to the roof and siding that are closer to what would have been on the house in the seventeenth century.

The Blake House is the oldest of the three houses proudly owned by the Dorchester Historical Society (another is discussed with building #4). In 1974, it was listed on the National Register and became one of the first individual properties in Boston to be designated a Landmark, in recognition of its national significance as a rare surviving seventeenth-century home and due to the rarity of its architectural construction techniques. Today, it is occupied year-round by a live-in caretaker who gives free monthly tours of the house. As it approaches its fourth century in existence, it remains a testament to Boston and Dorchester's colonial past, the region's historic architecture, and the efforts by many individuals that go into preserving the past.

# 2. Paul Revere House

19 North Square, North End | Ca. 1680

FIGURE 2.1

The Paul Revere
House around 1889,
when it still had
its complete third
floor and was sur-
rounded on both
sides by apartment
buildings (BPL
1898c; image cour-
tesy of the BPL).

After a devastating 1676 fire gutted North Square, many homes in the neighborhood were rebuilt as houses similar in scale and style to the Revere House.
It is not exactly clear when the house was built, but a November 1681 deed
documents Robert and Elizabeth Howard's purchase of the property with
a house on it.[1]

Robert Howard was a wealthy merchant, slave owner, and town selectman
who traded in the Caribbean, including Barbados, Jamaica, and Antigua.[2] The
house stayed in the Howard family until 1741, when it passed through the
ownership of Andrew Knox, a mariner, and then his son.[3] The son defaulted
on a mortgage with John Erving, a real estate speculator, but Erving allowed
Knox to stay on the property as a renter. By the middle of the eighteenth
century, one of the owners had added a third story and augmented the rear
of the property, greatly increasing the house's living space (figure 2.1).[4]

In 1770, Paul Revere purchased the house from Erving, moving into it with
his wife, Sarah; their five children; and his mother, Deborah.[5] After Sarah's
death in 1773, following the birth of their eighth child, Paul married Rachel
Walker. Of Paul's sixteen children with his two wives, five were born in the
1770s when the Revere family lived in the house.

It was from this house that Paul Revere departed on April 18, 1775, on the
famous midnight ride to Lexington with news that royal troops were heading

west from Boston. Though he owned the house until 1800, the family appears to have been living elsewhere in the 1780s, when the house was occupied by renters—including a tailor named George de France and a painter of miniatures named Joseph Dunkerly. Revere and his family returned to live in the house through the 1790s.[6]

After 1800, the house—already 120 years old—became a boardinghouse, and the first floor was converted into commercial space, housing a candy store, cigar factory, bank, fruit and vegetable stand, and other businesses.[7] Boston's population grew more than eightfold from 1820 to 1880, with more than 114,000 residents (one-third of the population) recorded as immigrants in the 1880 census.[8] This explosion of residents resulted in many of the North End's middle- and upper-middle-class families and investors converting their homes into rental units or tearing down their homes to make room for larger rental buildings.

From 1803 to 1867, the Loring family owned the house, and it was used as a boardinghouse for sailors.[9] In 1867, Catherine Wilkie purchased the property. She and her husband, James, both lived in the house and ran a boardinghouse there until 1891. Sidney Squires then purchased the property from the Wilkies, and he owned the house until 1902.[10] In 1902, Paul Revere's great-grandson, John P. Reynolds Jr., bought the building to keep it from being demolished to build larger and taller brick apartments and hotels, as many neighboring properties had been.[11] Along with other preservationists, business owners, and Revere descendants, Reynolds formed the Paul Revere Memorial Association, which oversaw the restoration of the house.

Much of what you see on the exterior of the house today is intended to resemble its seventeenth-century appearance. Despite modifications necessary after a hundred years of use as a rental property, the house retains nearly 90 percent of its original post and beam structure and significant portions of its seventeenth-century historic fabric—including several window frames and doors, the foundation, inner walls, portions of the roof, the basement fireplace, and much of the subflooring.[12] Joseph E. Chandler spearheaded the 1907–8 restoration (and would later restore building #7).[13]

Historic preservation is all about choices. Which appearance should be kept? Should it be the appearance of the building at its most significant period in history? The appearance that can be best documented to retain accuracy? The appearance of the building when it was purchased by an individual or group? Or the way the building looked originally? What if a decision was made but research reveals that that appearance is not attractive by today's standards or public opinion? There is no easy or correct answer to these questions, and the stewards of these properties must make these decisions and be held accountable for their actions by future preservationists, for better or worse. Chandler aimed to restore the building's exterior not to Paul Revere's residency during the Revolution, but to its appearance when it was built ca. 1680. Like the Blake House restoration seven years earlier, this restoration was based on the contemporary design trends and understandings of seventeenth-century architecture and design.

Chandler's most significant modification to the structure included eliminating the eighteenth-century enlargement made to the third story of the house, a space that served as rooms for several members of the Revere family. This modification did not change the overall height of the house, but it transformed the pitch of the front roof, reduced the living space, and removed four windows from the third floor.

After its restoration, the Paul Revere House opened to the public in 1908, becoming the one of the oldest house museums in the United States.[14] The Paul Revere Memorial Association remains the owner and caretaker of the Paul Revere House, the c. 1711 Pierce-Hichborn House (see building #5), and the recently purchased and renovated visitor center in the 1835, 5 and 6 Lathrop Place buildings. The buildings and courtyard create a visitor experience that features three centuries of Boston domestic architecture (figure 2.2). Though it remains one of the best cared for historic properties in Boston and its historical and architectural significance is clear, the city has not designated the Revere House a Landmark. However, it is a National Historic Landmark and has been on the National Register since 1961. One of the most popular historic homes in New England, today it welcomes hundreds of thousands of visitors a year.

FIGURE 2.2 A contemporary view of the rear of the Revere House and courtyard. A rear staircase was removed when the courtyard was renovated in 2016 to improve the site's accessibility. The modifications allowed for larger outdoor gathering spaces and made it possible to move between the Revere House and the new Education and Visitors Center in 5 and 6 Lathrop Place (located to the left of this image) (Paul Revere Memorial Association 2019; image courtesy of the association).

# 3. Pierce House

24 Oakton Avenue, Dorchester | 1683

c. 1683

c. 1712

c. 1765

FIGURE 3.1
Digital reconstruction of the Pierce House ca.1683, 1712, and 1765 (photo and edits by author).

Nestled within a neighborhood of single-family homes from the nineteenth and early twentieth centuries is the elongated Pierce House on Oakton Avenue. Its facade that faces the street strongly suggests the possibility that multiple homes existed within this one building, with two very prominent doorways present on the front of the house. The doors are remnants of a remarkable progression of building styles and additions to this building over hundreds of years, and the Pierce House is by far the best surviving example of how seventeenth- and eighteenth-century buildings evolved in Boston.

Robert Pierce was granted a six-acre lot in southern Dorchester in the mid-1600s.[1] Dendrochronological dating of one of the house's beams indicates that the earliest part of the building was constructed in 1683,[2] so Robert's son, Thomas, is likely to have paid for the house to be built. It would remain in the Pierce family for ten generations and nearly three centuries, until it was purchased in 1968 by the Society for the Preservation of New England Antiquities (SPNEA), now known as Historic New England.[3]

Unlike the older Blake House (see building #1), the Pierce House started its history as an asymmetrical building with a chimney and door placed on the left of a house with two and a half stories, containing a room on each floor and a gabled roof with a dormer for living space in the attic (figure 3.1). This asymmetrical layout allowed for additions to be made to the house when finances permitted, and around 1712 a room was added to the west side of the now-central chimney on each of the first and second floors.[4]

In the eighteenth century, Colonel Samuel Pierce Jr. resided in the house with his wife, Elizabeth Howe; their many children; and other members of the Pierce family.[5] While there, Samuel regularly recorded his daily life as a farmer in his journal. These firsthand accounts primarily focus on his crops, trade, and other farmers, but they also provide his perspective on the events leading up to the Revolution—including growing resentment of the king, Pierce's resignation from the royal militia and his joining the Massachusetts militia, and his involvement in the fortification of Dorchester Heights—through the lens of a Dorchester farmer.[6] His journal also includes notes on major events of the Revolution, such as the Boston Massacre (see building

#7), the battles at Lexington and Concord (see building #2), and Battle of Bunker Hill (see building #31).[7]

Samuel Pierce extensively renovated the house around 1765, near the time he inherited the property from his father in 1768.[8] It is likely that the renovations were executed by Samuel and his brother, Edward, who was a housewright.[9] These renovations and additions included adding a room to each floor on the eastern side of the house and adding a lean-to to the rear of the property. The lean-to turned what had been an exterior wall at the back of the house into an interior wall. The renovation retained the exterior clapboards on the former outside of the building, preserving what may be the only surviving seventeenth-century exterior wood clapboards in Boston and some of the oldest preserved exterior building elements in the country (figure 3.2).[10]

When Samuel finished the renovations on the house in 1765 and moved into the home with his new wife, Elizabeth, the newlyweds occupied the central portion of the building, while Samuel's parents lived in a new addition to the east. Samuel's three unwed sisters lived in the western portion of the building, which had been added around 1712. Together, the Pierce family lived in a kind of Boston three-decker turned on its side, with multiple members of the same family occupying different independent sections of a partitioned house. In the nineteenth century, the Pierce family added the eastern door and separated the eastern addition, turning it into a separate unit with a private entrance that was rented out to the family of a hired farm helper.

Samuel's additions to the interior included the Georgian paneling around the fireplace area. This has close similarities to the interior of the Lemuel Clap House (see building #4), which is not surprising as the Pierce and Clap families were friends, and Edward Pierce is likely to have worked on both Dorchester houses.[11]

Antoinette Pierce, a member of one of the last generations of the family to own the house, wanted the house to be given to a historical society or museum if the family was unable to keep the building. Her wish was carried out in 1968 when the house until it was sold to the SPNEA (figure 3.3). Though it listed on the National Register, the Pierce House has not been designated a Boston Landmark. Today, it is well maintained and protected by Historic New England, and it serves as both a museum and an educational space for dozens of school group visits each year.

FIGURE 3.2 View of the preserved seventeenth-century clapboards on the back of the Pierce House, which were protected by the addition of an eighteenth-century lean-to (Carmack 2010; image courtesy of HNE).

FIGURE 3.3 View of the Pierce House around 1898, while it was still owned by the Pierce family (BPL 1898d; image courtesy of the BPL).

# 4. Lemuel Clap House

199 Boston Street, Dorchester | Ca. 1710

Willow Court, now partially Enterprise Street, marks one edge of the rapidly evolving South Bay area. This road once led northwest of Boston Street toward the western end of South Bay, ending at a large tidal pond with a grist mill. This mill, which converted grain into flour, was owned by the Clap family starting in the seventeenth century. Their large family estate included much of the surrounding area up to Andrew Square, and the family's 1630s home was located on Willow Court. As of the writing of this book, the site of the seventeenth-century house is a Verizon office and parking lot, but it will soon be part of the South Bay shopping center. The Lemuel Clap House stood on this spot from its construction around 1710 until its move down the street to its current home, at 199 Boston Street.

In 1633, Roger Clap, one of the earliest English colonists in Dorchester, hired builders to construct a house for his family somewhere on Willow Court. It is possible that the 1633 foundations for the building were reused by the later Lemuel Clap House, and may be the former site of one of the earliest houses in Boston.[1]

The Clap estate was large, and its land was used for farming, mill work, and the cultivation of fruit trees—which was popular among Dorchester and Roxbury residents. Around 1710, perhaps due to a fire in the earlier house or just to expand the size of the home for their growing family, the Claps built a small one- or two-story home with a side chimney.[2] Today, the earliest portion of that building can be found in the central part of the Lemuel Clap House, in a room with considerably lower ceilings than the rest of the home.

One way to date portions of a house is to count the number of window panes, or lights, in an old window. Early windows had many more panes of

FIGURE 4.1
View of the Lemuel Clap House in its original setting from across Willow Court, around 1898 (BPL 1898e; image courtesy of the BPL).

glass than modern windows, as it has become much less difficult and expensive to create large sheets of glass. Windows in the seventeenth century were casements with side hinges and diamond-pane lights, as seen with buildings #1 and #2. Double-hung windows from the early eighteenth century that move up and down may have 9–12 lights in each sash. Architectural historians refer to types of windows by the number of lights in each sash, so a "twelve-over-twelve" (written "12/12") window has two sashes, each with twelve lights.

The Clap House has four original 12/12 windows, which likely date to the 1760s. Later in the Federal period, glaziers (people who build and install windows in houses) settled on 6/6 windows as the standard. This style can be seen in the remaining Clap House windows and the main structure of the William Clapp (who added a second *p* to the family name) House next door. In the mid-nineteenth century Greek Revival period, windows were typically 8/8, which can be seen in the rear addition behind the William Clapp House, and Victorian windows are 2/2, with a central muntin (the wood between the lights) running vertically through the sash. Original Victorian 2/2 windows can be seen in the three-decker homes across the street from the Clap House.

In the 1760s, Lemuel Clap, a member of the fifth generation of the family to own the property, greatly expanded the home, producing its current appearance by creating an L-shape house five bays (or openings) wide by three bays deep, with a gambrel roof with two distinct roof pitches typical of eighteenth-century Georgian architecture (figure 4.1).[3] Inside, the Georgian

FIGURE 4.2
Plan from 1937 showing buildings in the Lemuel Clap estate, including the L-shape Lemuel Clap House on the right (yellow)) and outbuildings on the left (blue) (Library of Congress [LOC] 1937; image courtesy of the Historic American Buildings Survey, edits by author).

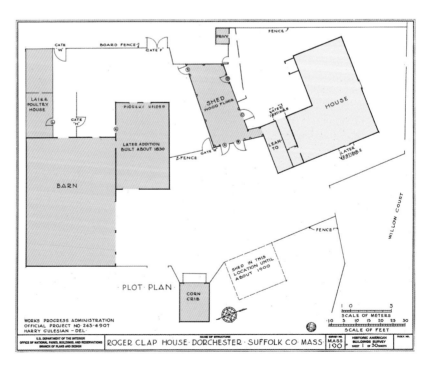

*1633 Clap House in process of being Moved Summer of 1957*

interior, probably created by Edward Pierce, survives and is remarkably similar to the parlor in the contemporary Pierce House (building #3).

Captain Lemuel Clap was a leader of the Dorchester militia during the Revolution.[4] He aided in the fortifications that were built across Boston Street near his home to prevent British troops from traveling south from the Dorchester Heights in South Boston.[5] During the Siege of Boston, the Lemuel Clap House—located just behind the fortifications on Boston Street—housed rebel troops.[6]

The house remained in the family until 1946, when Frank Lemuel Clapp sold the estate and its buildings to the Dorchester Historical Society (DHS) and became the house's first caretaker.[7] To fund the care and maintenance of the properties, the DHS sold the rear lot. After documenting the house's historic landscape and architectural elements (figure 4.2), the DHS moved the house in 1957 onto a new foundation in the former driveway of the 1806 William Clapp House, where it remains today (figure 4.3).

The Lemuel Clap House is listed on the National Register but is not a Boston Landmark. Today, the house is owned and maintained by the DHS and is occupied by a year-round live-in caretaker. It and the two other houses owned by the DHS, the Blake House (building #1) and William Clapp House, are open for tours once a month.

FIGURE 4.3
View down Willow Court (now partially Enterprise Street) in 1957, showing the Lemuel Clap House lifted off its original foundation and the prepared new foundation in foreground, where the house currently stands (Dorchester Historical Society [DHS] 1957; courtesy of the DHS).

# 5. Pierce-Hichborn House

29 North Square, North End | Ca. 1711

The Pierce-Hichborn House does not share all of the attention given to its neighbor to the north, the Paul Revere House (building #2). John Jeffs, a mariner, owned a home at the location of the Pierce-Hichborn House that burned down in the 1676 North Square fire.[1] His daughter, Mary Pierce, petitioned the town of Boston for permission to build a wooden home on the property in 1701 to replace her father's house.[2]

In December 1710 her son, Moses, purchased the property from his mother, which at the time contained stores occupied by his window glazing business.

FIGURE 5.1
View of front facade of the Pierce-Hichborn House from the front yard (photo by author).

Moses appears to have demolished the wooden building he had purchased and to have hired masons to construct a new brick home on the lot in 1711.[3] The house has Georgian styling typical of the early 1700s, including subtle brick arches above each window, a prominent "belt course" of bricks protruding from the facade between each floor, a shallow hipped roof, and two prominent chimneys on the back wall of the house instead of the central chimney common in earlier styles of buildings. The three-story house had slightly lower ceilings on the third floor. Judging by its scale, the upper floor may have contained servant quarters, though no en-slaved people or servants are listed in the Pierce probate records.

Moses Pierce chose to place his front door on the side of the house instead of on the street. The pre-1710 building that this house replaced was described as "facing Clarke's Square" (an early name for North Square), indicating that previous buildings on the site were oriented facing the square.[4] Because Pierce was a glazier—someone who builds and installs windows—he appears to have chosen a much wider and symmetrical front facade so that he could feature his large glass windows (figure 5.1). Essentially, Pierce designed an advertisement for his business.

Pierce sold the house in 1747, and it was eventually purchased by Nathaniel Hichborn in 1781.[5] Hichborn, a boat builder, was a cousin to his neighbor, Paul Revere (see building #2). The Pierce-Hichborn House would remain in the Hichborn family until it was sold in 1864.[6]

During the immigrant population boom in the North End in the nine-

FIGURE 5.2 The Pierce-Hichborn House in 1941, showing the building that partially filled the yard and the tunnel (behind the dog) that allowed access to the front of the house and the rear apartments (LOC 1941b; image courtesy of the Historic American Buildings Survey).

teenth century, the house was converted into apartments, with a shop on the first floor. At some point between 1843 and 1852, the owners added a two-story wood structure that filled the gap between the front of the house and the neighboring property (figure 5.2).[7] The addition included a tunnel or passageway that allowed access to the front door of the house from the street. The 1900 U.S. census records members of the Italian-born Ferullo, Giordana, and Delarocco families as living in the house.[8]

In 1941, the architect Carleton Richmond purchased the Pierce-Hichborn House, and a restoration headed by another architect, Charles R. Strickland, began in 1949.[9] This work removed the wooden addition along North Square and restored the interior and exterior of the building to its Georgian appearance (its present state). The Paul Revere Memorial Association took over the property in 1970 and uses the house as office space, offering occasional guided tours.[10]

Today, the Pierce-Hichborn House is the oldest brick house in Boston, and its skewed form and odd entrance placements demonstrate the creativity of early developers working within the constraints of early house lots along Boston's crooked streets. The building is within the pending North End Landmark District, is a National Historic Landmark, and has been on the National Register since 1968.

# 6. Ebenezer Clough House

21 Unity Street, North End  |  Ca. 1711

Ebenezer Clough, a master mason, laid out Unity Street after he and his wife, Thankful, purchased an undeveloped lot of land near the center of Boston's North End in 1711.[1]

There, he built a row of brick homes—including his own, at 21 Unity Street.[2] Originally, the house was two stories tall with five bays. Stylistically, it is a classic brick Georgian row house, though it boasts unique raised brick apron-like panels between the first and second floors.[3] Perhaps Clough was attempting to show off his skills in the construction of his own home.

Clough was widely known in Boston as a go-to person for building fine brick structures, and he is responsible for the construction of Old North Church (building #13) and was likely responsible for the building of other nearby brick structures, including the Pierce-Hichborn House (building #5) and the Union Oyster House (building #9). His buildings have stood the tests of time.

Just prior to Clough's death in 1724, the Ebenezer Clough House was divided into halves, with the south half going to one of his daughters, Susanna, and the north half to one of his sons, John.[4] In the same year, both children sold their halves to Jonathan Brown, a blacksmith who was also their brother-in-law.

On September 25, 1756, Brown sold the property,[5] and it was purchased later that year by Joseph Pierce, a mariner, and his wife, Sarah.[6] Pierce died two years later, and Sarah Pierce married Henry Roby, a glazier, in 1761. They were the last owner-occupants of the house.[7]

After Henry Roby's death in 1807, his wife's two daughters, Sarah and Mary Pierce, and their politically active husbands, Samuel Gore and Moses Grant,[8] added a third story to the house and converted it into a tenement with commercial space on the first floor (figure 6.1).[9] Both Grant and Gore were Sons of Liberty and participants in the Boston Tea Party.

In total, 180 different working-class families lived in the Clough House from 1809 until 1917, most for only one or two years at a time.[10] In the 1830 cen-

FIGURE 6.1 Digital reconstruction of the Clough House as a two-story building before the expansion in the early nineteenth century (photo and edits by author).

sus alone there were twenty-three people from five families sharing four rooms and an outdoor toilet at the house. These conditions were typical in the North End during this time (figure 6.2).

In 1944 the house was sold to the City of Boston, which planned to renovate the building and convert it into a museum. These plans did not materialize, and the property remained a rental property—housing a small number of renters throughout the mid-twentieth century as the house continued to fall into disrepair (figure 6.3).[11]

The abutting property, today an open space that is part of nearby Prado Park, once contained the home of Jane Franklin, Ben Franklin's sister, which was also built by Ebenezer Clough. The demolition of this building sparked interest in preserving the Clough House. In 1959, the Old North Church purchased the Clough House and restored it to its 1806 appearance. Today, the first floor of the home is open to the public, and its interior features numerous surviving eighteenth-century decorative elements. Though it is a National Historic Landmark and is associated with an important builder of eighteenth-century buildings in Boston and two participants in the Boston Tea Party, as well as having architectural rarity and significance, the Clough House is not a Boston Landmark.

# 7. Old State House

State Street, Downtown | 1713

The Old State House was built in 1713 after the original 1658 Town House burned down in 1711. The massive new brick building—118 by 36 feet—housed commercial space on the first floor, with the second floor containing the royal governor's Council Chambers, a courtroom, and the chamber of the publicly elected Massachusetts Assembly.[1] The three-part division of the executive, judicial, and legislative branches of government became a precursor to the structure of the future US government.[2]

With three and a half stories, as well as a prominent central wooden tower and lantern, the new Town House, today called the Old State House, was one of the tallest buildings in the city of Boston. Much of the brick exterior is original, but in 1747, a fire gutted the building and destroyed the original central tower.[3] Royal Governor William Shirley (see building #19) briefly considered relocating the colony's government to Roxbury or Cambridge in Massachusetts, or even to Maine—then territory of the Massachusetts Colony.[4] It was eventually decided to reuse the remaining brick shell in the 1748 rebuilding.

During the Revolution, the 1770 Boston Massacre took place in front of the building's eastern end (figure 7.1). Bostonians tore down and burned the lion and unicorn symbols of royal oppression, and the Declaration of Independence was first read in Massachusetts from the balcony on the building's its eastern end.[5]

The Town House became the Massachusetts State House in 1776 until the new State House opened on Beacon Hill in 1798.[6] In the nineteenth century, the building served as commercial space except for a brief stint as Boston's City Hall from 1830 to 1841. In 1831, the town replaced the early sundial on the east facade with a Simon Willard clock that still functions.[7] After City Hall departed, the merchants who now had full use of the building modified the entrances and interior of the structure and even expanded the roof to make more room for occupants.[8] By the 1880s, rampant commercialism within the building had transformed much of the exterior space into a large billboard advertising the merchants within (figure 7.2).

In 1876, the same year the nearby Old South Meeting House (building #16) faced demolition; plans were made to demolish

FIGURE 7.1

Paul Revere's etching of the Boston Massacre, with the east facade and the original sundial of the Old State House in the background (Revere 1770; image courtesy of the LOC).

the Old State House and replace it with larger office buildings. These plans were met with mixed reactions by Bostonians. The pro demolition movement was thwarted when the City of Chicago offered to dismantle and move the building to the shores of Lake Michigan after the devastating Chicago fire of 1871.[9] Distance made Boston hearts grow fonder, and the threat of Chicago's getting the building resulted in its staying put.

In 1881, the Bostonian Society was formed to preserve the Old State House. Recently renamed Revolutionary Spaces, the organization remains the caretakers and occupiers of the city-owned building. Since its stewardship began, three major restorations have taken place within the building.

In 1882, the architect George Clough began a restoration of the Old State House, using the 1830s plans for the City Hall conversion that included inaccurate Greek Revival interpretations of earlier Georgian styles.[10] In 1907, Joseph E. Chandler, who had recently completed his interpretative version of a colonial restoration at the Paul Revere House (see building #2), began a restoration of the Old State House. A 1943 restoration by the architectural firm Perry, Shaw, and Hepburn (which restored Colonial Williamsburg in Virginia) continued this interpretative work.

Together, the 1882, 1907, and 1943 restorers used contemporary tastes and designs that were looked upon favorably at the time rather than making well researched and more accurate restorations of the building to its original appearance.[11] One of the more visible aspects of these changes is the overemphasis restorers placed on using white paint to cover or "restore" what would have been the darker and more colorful original interiors of most spaces from the early and mid-eighteenth century.

On the exterior, most of the brick is original to 1713. The balcony and woodwork date mostly to the 1748 rebuilding after the fire, and the 1748 central tower is a larger replacement of the original. The iconic lion and unicorn statues are 2016-restored 1921 replacements of Clough's 1882 replicas of the 1776-burned 1747 replacements of the 1713 originals. The 1831 Simon Willard clock was restored in the 1990s, after the removal of the 1957 replica of the original sundial depicted in Paul Revere's etching of the Boston Massacre. The bulbous mansard roof was deflated back to its original gable during the 1882 Clough renovations.[12]

The longer north and south facades, which contain the main entrances, include Chandler's 1907 Colonial Revival entrances, which are more grandiose than their originals would have been. Finally, the more subdued eastern facade features gilded scrolls added during Clough's 1882 restoration and a fiberglass replica of the state seal first added by Clough. The large decoration of an eagle on a globe does not appear in depictions of the building from the mid-nineteenth century and was also probably added by Clough.[13]

The Old State House stands as an icon of both Boston's history and the history of historic preservation. Even though the changes brought about during the 1882, 1907, and 1943 restorations may have been somewhat inaccurate, they are still recognized as significant steps in preservation history and are now historically significant and worthy of preservation. The Old State House is a National Historic Landmark and a Boston Landmark.

# 8. Boston Light Station

Little Brewster Island, Boston Harbor Islands | 1716

The many islands in Boston's deep harbor posed a threat to navigation in the dark. Jasper Danker, a Dutchman touring the American colonies, documented the first known lighthouse in Boston on Little Brewster Island in 1679.[1]

Little Brewster belongs to a group of small, rocky islands on the eastern edges of Boston Harbor. They were named after the Brewster family of the *Mayflower* and Plimoth fame. Technically, the earliest documented beacon mentioned by Danker would have been located in the town of Hull, which owned the islands in the seventeenth century, but it had likely been in place for several decades by the time of its first mention. No further description of the early beacon is known, but it was probably a combination of a vessel or container containing a substantial fire, raised on some sort of pole or structure to increase its visibility.

In 1713, John George, a Boston merchant, successfully petitioned the General Court of the Massachusetts Colony (probably in the new Old State House—see building #7) for a larger beacon at the southern point of Beacon Island, as Little Brewster was known at the time. His petition was successful, and work began on the beacon in July 1714.[2]

The builders constructed the tower using stone rubble and put a small structure on top to hold a fire that was lit from sunset to sunrise each day (figure 8.1). On September 14, 1716, George Worthylake, the first keeper of the lighthouse, lit the beacon for the first time. George; his wife, Anne; their daughter, Ruth; their servant, George Cutler; and their enslaved man, Shadwell, were to live on the island year-round to maintain the light. Tragically, the Worthylake family, Cutler, Shadwell, and a friend of the family named John Edge drowned in 1718 when their boat capsized on the way back from church on the mainland.[3] The Worthylake family is buried under a triple headstone at Granary Burying Ground.

FIGURE 8.1 Drawing of the original Boston Light around 1730 (Burgis 1730; image courtesy of the LOC).

FIGURE 8.2
The dotted line in the image represents the approximate area below which the earliest 1716 component of the light survive (Linsdell 2013b; edits by author).

In 1720, the fire at the top of the tower got out of hand, causing damage to the overall structure—including large cracks in its stone walls.[4] The structure was soon damaged again, by a massive storm in 1723.[5] Still, the tower stood until the Revolution. In 1775, Boston rebels chose to burn down the upper parts of the structure to prevent British regulars from using it during the Siege of Boston. On March 17, 1776, all of Boston watched anxiously as the defeated British evacuated Boston for Nova Scotia. Though the fleeing ships did not burn Boston as they left, the did blow up Boston Light Station.[6]

Still needing a lighthouse, Bostonians raised a bucket of burning coal or wood to the top of a pole each night on the island for several years after. In 1780, Governor John Hancock requested the town to build a new lighthouse. Between 1780 and 1783 a new Boston Light Station was built on the ruins of the old, using the old twenty-five-foot-wide base and raising the rubble walls to seventy-five feet in height, with a fifteen-foot-tall lantern at the top to house the light. The new light had 161-gallon whale oil burners inside four separate lamps, giving it much greater visibility.[7]

In 1790, all lighthouses along the coast were formally ceded to the federal government. At the time of the transfer, Little Brewster Island included the light, a house for the lightkeeper, boathouse, storage shed, paint shed, and oil house.[8]

Boston Light remained in good condition for decades, but by 1809, iron rings, still visible today, were added to the tower as a support for the stone walls. The next major change occurred in 1856, when the lantern was upgraded to increase its visibility to sixteen miles. The structure took its current and final form in 1859 when the tower was increased to a height of ninety-eight feet, and the lantern was upgraded so that it spins.[9] Most recently, the tower was restored ahead of its three hundredth anniversary by the US Coast Guard.[10] During this renovation, the original 1716 elements of the building were documented, proving that the original tower survives as part of the current structure (figure 8.2).[11] It is kept by Sally Snowman, a civilian, and it remains the last staffed lighthouse in the country.

In May 2020, the US General Services Administration announced that it was interested in transferring the stewardship of Boston Light to a new owner.[12] Though it is a National Historic Landmark, it is not a Boston Landmark.

# 9. Union Oyster House

41–43 Union Street, Downtown | Ca. 1716

FIGURE 9.1
View of the Union
Oyster House around
1860 (BPL 1860c;
image courtesy of
the BPL).

FIGURE 9.2
View of the Union
Oyster House around
1920 (BPL 1920;
image courtesy of
the BPL).

The Union Oyster House opened in 1826 and boasts the title of the country's oldest restaurant in continuous operation.[1] You have to stand almost in the memorial park across the street to see the entire building (and hope there isn't a beer delivery truck blocking the view), but from there you will be able to see the full three stories of the building—likely built by Ebenezer Clough, who also built his own house (see building #6) and others in this book. From afar, the Union Oyster House has a slightly odd shape as it spans a bend in the seventeenth-century Union Street. It was not always that way, though.

The large historic windowed storefronts form the first floor of the restaurant. The second- and third-floor windows are often covered by awnings, but they contain 12/12 windows from the nineteenth century that replaced the 6/6 originals. The fourth story, an attic with three gables, is clad with a slate roof.

In the early 1700s, the tailor John Savell began to purchase multiple lots on Union Street between Marsh Lane and Marshall Street.[2] One of these was bought in 1713 from none other than Clough, though the property did not have the current brick house on it.[3] In September 1717, Savell sold this lot to John Green, a cooper, with a "new built brick messuage or tenement."[4] Given the connection between Clough and the property, it is highly likely that he had been hired by Savell to construct the building.

After passing through multiple owners, the property was purchased by Hopestil Capen, a dealer in fine clothing, in the late 1700s. With his wife, Patience Stoddard, he opened a shop in the house under the "Sign of the Cornfields." His son Thomas, and then Thomas's heirs, owned the house well into the twentieth century. The shop closed in 1826, with the opening of the Atwood and Bacon Oyster House—which was quickly renamed the Union Oyster House restaurant.[5]

From the exterior, several periods of the house's history are visible. The majority of the brickwork is original, and most of the chimney on the north wall and its interior stone base are original. The belt course and slightly arched windows on the second floor are nearly identical to those at the Pierce-Hichborn House (see building #5). The roof probably began in the gable style (with a single slope), but it was probably converted into the current gambrel (with a double slope) in the mid-eighteenth century when the original dormer windows and dental molding (small tooth-shape blocks of wood spaced at regular intervals) under the cornice roofline were also added.

The angled bend in the building is not original. If you look closely, you will see that the eighteenth-century belt course and the arches above the second-floor windows end at the bend. The original house would have continued in a straight line along Union Street for these two bays. In the mid-nineteenth century, Marshall Street was made six feet wider, requiring part of the Union Oyster House to be cut off. From 1852 to 1857 these two bays were rebuilt, triggering a renovation to the interior that brought in the current mahogany oyster bar, soapstone shucking bench, and the interior booths (figure 9.1).[6]

After this remodeling, the dormers, which had been removed, were returned to their original location in the 1930s. In addition, capitalizing on a revival of the Colonial Revival movement of the early twentieth century, the second-floor dining area was transformed into a faux colonial interior space (figure 9.2).[7]

The streets and sidewalks in the Blackstone Block, where the Union Oyster House stands, are Boston Landmarks. This piece of Boston's early architectural history survived for several reasons. The first is that it was large and made of brick, which made it not only strong and fire resistant, but also able to satisfy the needs of a growing city without being demolished due to its size. When building boomed again in Boston at the end of the nineteenth century and in the early twentieth, the property already contained a restaurant that was nearly a hundred years old and had no intentions on leaving. As it is still large enough to satisfy the needs of hordes of tourists, due in part to extensions to the rear of the original structure, it still remains. The Union Oyster House is a National Historic Landmark but not a Boston Landmark.

# 10. Ebenezer Smith House

15–17 Peaceable Street, Allston-Brighton | Ca. 1716

The Ebenezer Smith House is located on a quiet street in the Brighton section of the Allston-Brighton neighborhood of Boston, surrounded by the nineteenth- and twentieth-century single- and multi-family homes that are common throughout the area.

The house is a modest two-story structure with a gabled roof, raw wood shingles, and a prominent two-story bay window on its western end, which sits on a brick foundation. The rear of the building has a two-story lean-to addition, and there is a small projecting entryway on the front and side of the building.

Brighton was originally part of Cambridge and was referred to as Little Cambridge. This also placed Brighton in Middlesex County until it was annexed by Boston.

Deeds show that Ebenezer Smith was the first owner of the building and remained there throughout most of the eighteenth century.[1] Smith was born in 1688 in Brighton and funded the construction of a new house for himself sometime around 1716, when he bought two hundred acres of land in the area.[2] Despite this large acreage, the house once projected into the road, leading one Brighton resident, whose recollections of the old house were recorded, to remark that it seemed illogical that someone would build their house practically in the road when they had so much open space in which to put it.[3] When the house was built, the commercial center of Brighton, as it is today, was located just to the north, at the corner of Market and Washington Streets.

Smith died unmarried and childless in 1776 at the age of eighty-five. He left the house and his land to Ebenezer Smith Fowle and George Sparhawk, the sons of his cousins, but he stipulated in his will that the men must attend college or the inheritance would be forfeited.[4]

Jonathan Winship purchased the house from Fowle and Sparhawk in 1778.[5] During the Revolution, Winship was in charge of supplying food for the continental troops, and later he was responsible for promoting and increasing the cattle market and industry in Brighton.[6] He stayed in the Ebenezer Smith House only while his house was being built and promptly left when it was finished. At the end of the eighteenth century, the Reverend John Foster and his wife, Hannah, lived in the property for about five years.[7] You will be hearing about Hannah again with building #38.

In 1852, Cephas Bracket purchased the house and moved it back from its location partially in the street and onto a new brick foundation.[8] He also had the house lifted and the large central brick chimney replaced with a smaller version, as well as dividing the house into two units—which included removing the original front door.[9]

Since that time, a large bay window was added to the house, probably during the end of the nineteenth century, in an effort to have it better fit in with its Victorian neighbors. Because the house was similar in scale to its neighbors, it has not been chosen for demolition due to being too small or too big. The sale of the surrounding property allowed neighborhood housing to develop around the house, and its relocation back from its original footprint likely saved it from demolition in the late nineteenth and early twentieth centuries just for being in the way. Overall, this house has survived simply because it never drew much attention to itself once it was moved out of the road. The building is well cared for with fresh siding, but it is not on the National Register or Landmark designated. Today, this unassuming double home on a quiet street in Brighton stands as the oldest house in the Allston-Brighton neighborhood and one of the oldest in Boston.

When Ebenezer Clough purchased land in the area in a bit of a speculative buying spree in 1708 and 1711, he laid out the street that would become Unity Court and began building brick houses on it, including his own (see building #6).

In 1716, it appears that Clough ran out of steam and decided to sell one of his undeveloped parcels at the corner of Tileston Street (then Love Lane) and Unity Court to Ebenezer Kimball—like Clough, a bricklayer—and Kimball's brother, Jonathan.[1] Ebenezer Kimball extended the partial row of brick row houses built by Clough on Unity Street to the corner, building the house that partially remains today.

Deeds throughout the eighteenth century describe this property as the "southern half" of a house on the street.[2] This description reveals that the Kimball-Cheever House and the neighboring Parker-Emery House were seen as two halves of the same building. Historic drawings of the Parker-Emery House show that it was a "sideways house" like the nearby Pierce-Hichborn House (see building #5), with its main entrance located on the side of the building and its side facing the street. This suggests that in the eighteenth century, the Kimball-Cheever House had an entrance on Tileston, with its side facing Unity Street, and that it and the Parker-Emery House were oriented back-to-back.

FIGURE II.I
View down Unity Street in 1898, showing the Kimball-Cheever House at the end of the road after having undergone a partial demolition and rebuilding (BPL 1898f; image courtesy of the BPL).

The Kimball-Cheever House property passed on to Jonathan Kimball, alone, and remained in his possession until he sold it in 1741. In 1747 it was purchased by Joshua Cheever.[3]

Cheever, a wealthy and powerful Bostonian, was sixty years old when he and his wife, Sarah, moved into the house. Cheever was a Boston selectman and commander of the Ancient and Honorable Artillery Company.[4] Cheever died in 1751, leaving a massive estate of nearly 50,000 pounds—more than $2 million in today's money. Cheever left most of his estate to his wife but stated that Sarah's son from her first marriage, David Jenkins, was to receive the estate after Sarah's death.[5]

Like many wealthy families in Boston prior to the 1780s, the Cheevers were also enslavers. We know of two enslaved Africans who resided at 43 Tileston Street. Marriage records from Boston in the 1740s indicate that Jack,

an enslaved servant of Joshua Cheever, married first Flora, an enslaved servant of Captain Jonathan Snelling in 1741, and then Jenny, an enslaved servant of the Reverend Joshua Gee of Boston's Second Church in 1743.[6] Via the directions in Cleever's will, after his death, Jack was released from his enslavement and given forty ounces of silver to start his new life. However, Cheever also gave Spencer, an enslaved child, to his wife, Sarah, "to be at her own disposal forever."[7]

During the late nineteenth century, a fourth floor was added to the house, which was heavily rebuilt—possibly after a fire. This left only a small portion of the original first- and second-floor brickwork (figure 11.1).

Today, what remains of the original house is the first and partial second floor of the facade facing Unity Street. The bold belt course and English bond bricks with their alternating long-short pattern change abruptly near the top of the second-floor windows (figure 11.2). You can see the infilling along the windows and what appears to have been a door, most notably on the first floor—which now has dramatically smaller windows than it once did. The corner of the building shows the change from English to running bond bricks, which continues around the corner to the end of the property. Newer brick appears along its Tileston Street facade.

The house has been altered almost beyond recognition, indicating how heavily some old buildings have been modified to suit the changing needs of their owners and neighborhoods. Despite these modifications, the city block outlined by Unity, Tileston, Charter, and Salem Streets contains one of Boston's densest concentrations of brick structures from the early eighteenth century. Most of the North End is a pending Boston Landmark Historic District. The Kimball-Cheever House is not listed on the National Register and is not a Boston Landmark.

FIGURE 11.2 View of the first two floors of the south facade of the Kimball-Cheever House, showing the outline (yellow dots) of the original eighteenth-century components of the building (photo and edits by author).

# 12. Old Corner Bookstore

283 Washington Street, Downtown | 1718

FIGURE 12.1

View down School
Street from
Washington Street
in 1920, showing
the Old Corner
Bookstore at the
corner and the
5, 7, and 11 School
Street additions
to the building
(Abdalian 1920b;
image courtesy of
the BPL).

Thomas Crease purchased an old home and house lot at the corner of School
and Washington Streets in 1708. The house was the former home of William
Hutchinson and his controversial wife, Anne Hutchinson, who were banished
from Boston in 1637 due to Anne's allegedly heretical preaching. Just three
years later, Crease lost it in the great fire of 1711 that burned the nearby Town
House (see building #7).[1] His new brick house, built in 1718, still retains its
distinct eighteenth-century Georgian brick belt courses between each floor,
enlarged block-like quoins at its corners, and a broad double-angled gambrel
roof. The house fronts the old road to Roxbury—later called Orange and
then Washington Street—which was the primary overland trade route in
Boston. Accordingly, the first floor of the building was designed as a store
and originally housed Crease's apothecary, with his private residence above.[2]

In 1828, Timothy Carter began leasing the storefront for a publishing
house. Carter's brother, Richard, and friend, Charles Hendee, installed the
projecting windows facing the street. Carter expanded the property by con-
structing buildings at 5, 7, and 11 School Street, using the first floor of the
buildings as rental space and retail and the upper floors for publishing and
bookselling (figure 12.1).[3]

In 1833, John Allen and William D. Ticknor of the book publishing company Allen & Ticknor took over the buildings. The company would remain

owners until 1865 under the names William D. Ticknor (1834–43); William D. Ticknor & Co. (1843–48); Ticknor, Reed & Fields (1849–54); and Ticknor and Fields (1854–64).[4] The Old Corner Bookstore gained a reputation as a meeting place for writers. The corner of School and Washington Streets became known as Parnassus Corner after the ancient Greek home of the muses, where—according to myth—poetry, music, and learning were created.[5]

In 1859, Ticknor and Fields bought the *Atlantic Monthly*, further increasing the number of the company's major publications. This small storefront became the outlet for numerous authors—especially the transcendentalists, who flourished in the 1840s through the 1860s. Authors published by Ticknor and Fields and in the *Atlantic Monthly* included Henry David Thoreau, Harriet Beecher Stowe, Louisa May Alcott, Henry Wadsworth Longfellow, and Nathaniel Hawthorne. These authors released such well-known titles as *Uncle Tom's Cabin*, *Walden*, and *The Scarlet Letter* through the publishers in the Old Corner Bookstore.

In 1865, the company's size had outgrown the small space, and it departed.[6] Over the ensuing decades, other publishers and newspapers would leave the area, taking with them its association with the writing world. Yet the Old Corner Bookstore remained host to booksellers in the nineteenth and twentieth centuries, in addition to cigar shops, barbershops, hat stores, and other businesses (figure 12.2).

As Boston faced economic uncertainty throughout the mid-twentieth century, demolishing older buildings was seen as a way to allow new construction and expansion during the period of urban renewal. The relatively small building on a major downtown intersection was threatened with demolition in 1960 to make way for a new parking garage. In the same year, a group of Boston residents formed Historic Boston Incorporated (HBI) and purchased the billboard-covered Old Corner Bookstore and the neighboring Andrew Cunningham House (see building #15) (figure 12.3).

The nonprofit HBI fully restored the building to its 1828 publishing house

FIGURE 12.2 View of the exterior of the Old Corner Bookstore around 1900 (LOC 1900; image courtesy of the LOC).

appearance and converted the interior spaces of the buildings for retail. Today, still owned by HBI, the building is entirely leased to commercial entities, and the money raised through these leases helps fund the maintenance of the building and historic preservation at other endangered properties owned and being renovated by HBI.[7]

The Old Corner Bookstore is a Massachusetts Historic Landmark and listed on the National Register. It was nominated as a Boston Landmark in the late 1990s and has reached the Study Report phase of the Landmarking process, making it a pending Landmark.

# 13. Old North Church

191 Salem Street, North End | 1723

Old North Church, or Christ Church in the City of Boston, is the oldest standing church in the city. While no one knows who the architect for the church was, or even if there was one, it appears that the overall design is based on similar church designs by the British architect Sir Christopher Wren.[1] The architect William Price designed the original steeple, which was added seventeen years after the main structure was completed. Price was a Boston book and print dealer and is known to many scholars of Boston's history as the publisher of a 1743 map of the city, which was revised and reissued over multiple decades by John Bonner (see building #26).[2]

From 1723 to 1737, masons including Ebenezer Clough (see building #6) laid the hundreds of thousands of Medford clay bricks that make up the walls of Old North, which are several feet thick. When the steeple was added in 1740, it was crowned with a swallow-tailed weathervane by Shem Drowne, a metalworker and deacon of the church, and the total height of the building was raised to over 150 feet.[3]

Originally, Old North had two side entrances flanking its steeple. These were later removed to allow for more pews to be built and sold. The church was originally Anglican and was founded by a group of parishioners after the original Anglican Church, King's Chapel (see building #21), could no longer accommodate the growing congregation. At the time, King's Chapel was a much smaller, wooden version of its current granite form. The congregation chose a vacant plot of pasture on Salem Street for the site of its new church.[4]

The interior of the church has changed little over the years, except for the relatively new white paint. Recent forensic paint analysis has revealed the original presence of colorful painted cherubs in the arches of the ceiling (figure 13.1). When future restorations occur, these will probably be restored, which will be a dramatic change from the current stark-white interior. Though the pews are mostly original wood, their interiors have changed over time as individual owners decorated and furnished their pews as they saw fit.

Above the main entrance is the 1759 Thomas Johnston organ (figure 13.1), the second organ installed in the church, which retains several of its original eighteenth-century components. Flanking the organ on the second-floor gallery are several sculptures. In 1746, four wooden angels carved in the early 1600s were stored aboard a French ship bound for Quebec, where they were intended to be given to a newly established Catholic convent. Captain Thomas Gruchy, a British privateer, captured the ship (King George II had given privateers permission to capture foreign ships during the war with France). Gruchy took the contents of the ship back to his home port of Boston to be sold, but he felt that Old North—where he was a congregant—was the most appropriate location for the angels. They have remained in place ever since.[5]

During the Siege of Boston, the leader of the British occupying forces, General Thomas Gage, hatched a plan to march to the town of Concord to seize a large amount of gunpowder and arms and limit the ability of the rebel forces to defend themselves. Spies spread word of this plan, and Boston patriots—including Paul Revere and dozens of others—agreed to ride ahead of the British troops when the signal was given to alert townspeople that the troops were on their way. There were only two likely routes from Boston Common to Concord: via land, down Boston Neck into Roxbury, and the much faster route via sea, rowing the short distance across the Charles River and Back Bay to Cambridge.

On April 18, 1775, seven hundred British troops began their departure from Boston via boat. In response, the sexton of Old North, Robert Newman, and Revere's friend, Captain John Pulling Jr., climbed the steeple of Old North and lit two lanterns in the upper windows to signal that the British were taking the sea route. These lanterns were lit for only one minute, but the signal was successful, triggering William Dawes and Revere to depart and leading other riders to alert area residents of the impending troop advancement.

After the Revolution, the church became part of the new Protestant Episcopal Church in the United States, and it remains Episcopalian today. In 1804, a major storm knocked down the original Price steeple. Charles Bulfinch, the omnipresent architect of Boston in the early nineteenth century, is credited with designing its replacement. The Bulfinch steeple blew down in 1954 during Hurricane Carol and was rebuilt using the original 1740 Price design. Now 175 feet tall, Old North still bears its original, though often repaired, Drowne weathervane (figure 13.2).[6]

Until the early 1990s, the property was owned and maintained by the church.[7] The building is still owned by the church, but in 1991, the Old North

FIGURE 13.2
A mid-nineteenth-
century lithograph,
showing the
exterior of Old
North Church at
the time (BPL 1845;
image courtesy of
the BPL).

Foundation formed as a secular nonprofit organization with the responsibility to preserve the building and provide public education on the property's history. The foundation operates tours within the church, grounds, other properties on the campus, including the Ebenezer Clough House (see building #6), and in the church's crypt. For readers west of the Mississippi, there is a near-exact replica of Old North that can be visited at Forest Lawn Memorial Park cemetery in Hollywood Hills, California.

Old North is a National Historic Landmark and in 2019 began the process of becoming a Boston Landmark. The sustained efforts of its congregation and the historic preservation movement have allowed the church to remain a prominent part of Boston's history and skyline.

# 14. Daniels-Goldsmith House

266 Poplar Street, Roslindale | Ca. 1725

When it was first built around 1725 by the Chamberlain family, this house was in the town of Roxbury. It began its life as a half-cape, a style of Cape Cod architecture with a door and chimney on the right end (when you face the entrance) and the windows on the left that create an asymmetrical front facade similar to the original form of the Pierce House (see building #3). This starter house form allowed the owners to expand the building on the opposite side of the entrance and chimney when funds and the growth of their family allowed for or required it.

To make later expansions easier, when the central chimney was constructed, many builders would design into the chimney the future fireplaces for the as-yet-unbuilt portion of the house. It is this expandability that allowed earlier homes to survive for so long. Because they were designed and placed in lots with expansion in mind, they were able to be adapted to the changes in their use over time—at least until urbanization required lot-filling dense structures to accommodate city populations.

The house was expanded around 1775, adding three additional bays on the right side of the entry and resulting in its final appearance with a central door and chimney. The windows, which were probably smaller in the original house, were enlarged in that expansion, but the heavy summer beam (the primary load-bearing support) remains in the earlier portion.[1]

The house was renovated in the middle of the nineteenth century. It is likely that this renovation coincided with the purchase of the house by Henry L. Goldsmith from Richard Daniels in 1842, during the height of the Greek Revival period.[2]

The characteristics of Greek Revival architecture in its high form include columns, a temple-like appearance, and a prominent pediment. Pediments are triangular roofs with distinct lintels across the bottom of the roofline that separate the roof from the rest of the house, creating an effect similar to a child's drawing of a house as a triangle on top of a square. In rural areas, the Greek Revival style was a bit more subdued, and it can be seen in slightly wider windows with eight glass panes in each sash (8/8), partial or complete horizontal trim at the ends of gables that separate the roof and walls, and front doors with windows on either side called sidelights. See buildings #37 and #40 for dramatic examples of Greek Revival alterations to historic homes.

The most visible Greek Revival modification to the Daniels-Goldsmith House was the addition to the front entrance of sidelights, the long windows on either side of the door that are typical of this style of architecture. An 1886 plan shows an elongated ell behind the house to a former outbuilding and a separate structure on the property, probably a carriage house or barn.[3]

The latest addition to the house, in 1932, included a dormer at the rear of the building.[4] All of the outbuildings are now gone.

The relatively late arrival of urbanization to this area allowed the house to remain while land around it was sold off for development. Many older Boston houses sit on relatively large lots, which are attractive to developers and can often result in the demolition of an old house that is seen as in the way. However, it is possible to preserve historic structures on these properties by moving them or incorporating them into the design with some creativity on the part of developers.

The Daniels-Goldsmith House is not a Boston Landmark, nor does it have any state or federal historic designations. As it stands, this house is well loved and cared for by its current owner, who clearly values its historic character and setting. There are no risks to the home's preservation for the foreseeable future.

# 15. Andrew Cunningham House

277 Washington Street, Downtown  |  1728

Ironically overshadowed by its shorter neighbor, the Old Corner Bookstore (see building #12), the Andrew Cunningham House has its own unique history. The Cunningham family called this building home for three generations, beginning with Andrew, a glazier (window maker). His father, also a glazier named Andrew, is credited with mending the windows of an earlier version of King's Chapel (see building #21).[1]

The younger Andrew hired masons to build this house in 1728 in the style of a Georgian row house, immediately next to the slightly older 1718 Crease House (which became the Old Corner Bookstore; see building #12), both on the lot formerly owned by William and Anne Hutchinson.[2] The great fire of 1711 had erased the Hutchinson home and led to the predominance of the fire-resistant brick construction of the homes and businesses along Orange (now Washington) Street and in the surrounding area.

This house features a now-familiar eighteenth-century belt course of bricks that span the facade at each floor transition, where the floor joists inside the building connect to the brick walls. The three-and-a-half-story building has two dormers on the front of its gambrel roof, whose upper angled portion of the roof-line is difficult to see from the street.

FIGURE 15.1
View of the Cunningham House around 1865 (Hawes 1865; image courtesy of the BPL).

The building's primary and original use as a town house changed around 1795, due to increasing mercantilism along the busy Washington Street. This growth in mercantilism increased the demand for commercial spaces along the street, which was the only corridor for transportation via land in and out of Boston. The home's first floor was converted into a shop, which at the time was owned by John West, a publisher—further expanding Parnassus Corner, the publishing and writing hub centered on the intersection of Washington and School Streets at the beginning of the nineteenth century.[3]

West's modification included the expansion of the street-level windows into large shop displays for his books and paper goods. Throughout the nineteenth century, the first-floor shop and upper-floor living spaces had numerous occupants. The shop was divided in the early nineteenth century into two smaller shops, and by the middle of the nineteenth century the entire

FIGURE 15.2 View of the Cunningham House around 1965, showing the drastic alterations to and removal of much of its exterior fabric (Cushing 1965; image courtesy of HNE).

building was occupied by Jenks, Hickling, and Swan, a publisher of school books.[4]

Numerous drawings and photos of the more famous Old Corner Bookstore inadvertently document the changes at the Cunningham House since the nineteenth century (figure 15.1). The two original dormers on the fourth floor had been combined by the late nineteenth century, and like many of the buildings along Washington Street, all of the house's surfaces were covered in bold signs advertising the businesses and goods located within.

By 1960, changes to the building had removed almost all of its original facade (figure 15.2). In that year, Historic Boston Incorporated (HBI) purchased the Cunningham House and the Old Corner Bookstore. A stationer who had occupied the property for decades worked under the guidance of HBI in the 1970s to restore the historic facade based on historic photos. The Cunningham House and the Old Corner Bookstore are the only contiguous examples of Georgian town houses in Boston.

Today the property is not a designated Boston Landmark, nor does it have state or federal historic designations. However, it is still owned by HBI and leased as income-producing rental property to support of the nonprofit organization's historic preservation efforts.

# 16. Old South Meeting House

308 Washington Street, Downtown | 1729

FIGURE 16.1
View of the interior
of the Old South
Meeting House
around 1880, show-
ing the orientation
of the pulpit to
the congregation.
The image shows
the property being
used as a museum
shortly after it was
saved from demo-
lition in 1876 (BPL
1880a; image cour-
tesy of the BPL).

Nestled within downtown Boston and surrounded by commercial structures, including buildings #12 and #15 across the street, this 1729 meetinghouse replaced an earlier 1669 wooden church on the site called the Cedar Meeting House. The new two-and-a-half-story Georgian brick building with its prominent central spire has a slightly older seventeenth-century-style meetinghouse interior. Unlike Old North Church (see building #13) and King's Chapel (building #21), Old South does not have its pulpit on the opposite end of the spire or entrance but to the north (left) of the entrance, which makes for a wide and shallow meeting space that feels more like a concert hall than a church (figure 16.1). Like most other early Boston churches, the interior is currently white due to the covering of earlier, more colorful original paint because of the Colonial Revival tastes of late nineteenth and early twentieth centuries.

The design for the building is often credited to Robert Twelves, but since there are no primary documents to support this claim, the architect is probably unknown. The building includes the classic brick belt courses visible on most of brick buildings from the early eighteenth century, and it still has its original steeple.[1]

The builders planned to include a central public clock on the brick portion of the building's iconic octagonal spire, but a clock was not added to the structure until 1770. The 1776 Gawen Brown Clock, with its signed mechanism, remains the oldest working tower clock in the nation.[2]

Predating the clock, a bell had been installed in the church by 1731, but it cracked while ringing a fire alarm in 1815. The cracked bell was quickly sold for scrap and replaced in 1816 by a London-built bell that remained until 1875—when it too broke.[3] Old South would remain without a bell until a major renovation of the building that began in 2009 and included restoring the Brown clock and replacing the bell with a Paul Revere and Son bell donated by a church in Westborough, Massachusetts. This bell, installed in 2011, rang out from Old South for the first time in 2012.[4]

Old South was the location for many rallies and public meetings during the Revolution, and it was in its pews that rebels held a rally on December 16, 1773, at which Samuel Adams, John Hancock, and others spoke out against the tea tax and called on Bostonians to revolt. After a signal given by Adams, a group of rebel Sons of Liberty, dressed as Native people, marched to the wharves and destroyed 342 chests of tea by dumping them into Fort Point Channel. The event became known as the Boston Tea Party.

Unlike Old North, Old South did not remain intact during the Siege of Boston that followed. In 1775, General John Burgoyne, who was stationed in Boston during the war, ordered that the pulpit, pews, and all interior structures be torn out of the church. The open space was converted into a riding school for the King's Cavalry, an act seen by the Boston public as sacrilegious and insulting.

British troops and Tories evacuated Boston in 1776, and the interior of the meetinghouse was restored in 1783. The church's function as a meeting place and place of worship continued throughout much of the remaining eighteenth and early nineteenth centuries. It narrowly escaped the massive Great Boston Fire of 1872, whose rampant destruction of Boston's downtown stopped less than one block from the building (figure 16.2). Old South was saved from fire due to its brick and slate construction and a protective layer of wet blankets applied by townspeople to spare the structure.

FIGURE 16.2 Bostonians struggle to save the Old South Meeting House as fires rage nearby in 1872 (BPL 1900b; image courtesy of the BPL).

With the filling in of Back Bay, many of Boston's elite residents and a significant portion of Old South's congregation began to move toward the Victorian mansions and fashionable new buildings being built there. In 1874, the congregation moved into the new Gothic Revival–style "New" Old South Church on Boylston Street, and Old South was no longer used for religious purposes.

FIGURE 16.3
Banners on Old
South Meeting
House in 1876
ask for public
support to stop
the demolition
of the building
(Black 1876; image
courtesy of the BPL,
edits by author).

Despite the great efforts during the fire to save the building, it was soon threatened again. Having lost its original religious and social purposes, the building, then a post office, was slated for demolition (figure 16.3). The details of this and the resulting efforts to save the building are included in the introduction to this book, but in short, the Old South Association—Boston's first historic preservation group, founded in 1876—managed to raise the funds necessary to save the building.[5]

An innovative approach to historic preservation included the 1903 construction of the Old South Building immediately next door to Old South on the meetinghouse's land. This tall building is partially visible to the left of the church in the main image for this chapter. The funds from this building were placed in trust, in part to fund the preservation and maintenance of Old South.[6] The church is a National Historic Landmark, and in March 2020, it began the process of becoming a Boston Landmark. The Old South Building next door is also a pending Boston Landmark. Today, Old South is part of the new Revolutionary Spaces organization, a merger of the Bostonian Society (see building #7) and the Old South Association. The building functions as a museum and a place for public events. Its location along Boston's Freedom Trail ensures that it receives hundreds of thousands of yearly visitors.

# 17. Grant House

350 Hanover Street, North End | Ca. 1734

During my initial research for this book, the Grant House was listed in state records as being built around 1814 based on a map, with a comment that the building could date from the eighteenth century.[1] I first noticed this building's partial belt course on Tileston Street (figure 17.1) while I was photographing other buildings for this book, and that led me to deed research that revealed the true age of the house.

In 1734, John Grant, a carpenter, purchased at auction a parcel of land with an "Old House" on it from Deborah Love. She was the widow of Bennett Love, a bookbinder, and she needed to sell the land to pay off her husband's debts.[2] Grant married his wife, Elizabeth, later that year, which suggests that he purchased the land to build a new house on it for his future family.

The reference to the existing house as "old" in 1734 strongly suggests that there was a seventeenth-century home on the site when Grant bought it, and that the current building probably replaced that house soon after Grant purchased the lot.

The house appears to have stayed in the Grant family for most of the eighteenth century. In 1776, John willed his home to his three daughters, to be divided among them. As a result, the north and south halves of the home were divided among the daughters, and Grant's son, John Jr., inherited his father's carpentry business. The southern half of the property went to Sarah and Hannah Grant, and the northern half (the side facing the corner of Hanover and Tileston) went to Abigail Grant Hingston. Grant's probate records describe a house that had not previously been divided being separated into two living spaces, with new basement stairs added and closets and entrances shared by the sisters and their families.[3]

The house remained divided between two owners for some time. Abigail Hingston willed her northern half to the four sons of her brother, John. At the end of the eighteenth century, Levi Lane, a sailmaker, purchased the

FIGURE 17.1
View of belt course on the Tileston Street side of the Grant House (photo by author).

southern half of the house in 1795 from the heirs of Sarah and Hannah Grant,[4] and William Ward, a mariner, purchased the northern half from the Grant brothers in 1798.[5] The Ward family purchased Lane's half of the property in the early nineteenth century, and though the house remained divided internally,

FIGURE 17.2
A 1730 notice of Paul Revere Sr.'s move to either the Grant House property or the neighboring property (*Weekly News-Letter* 1730; image courtesy of Harvard University Library, edits by author).

the Wards continued to own it into the twentieth century, a remarkably long ownership for a North End property.

Around the beginning of the twentieth century, atlases show the addition of wooden storefronts onto the front facade of the brick building, which sits back a bit more from the sidewalk than most buildings on Hanover Street (it is by far the oldest building on the street). Throughout the twentieth century, the property remained a combination of storefront along Hanover Street and living spaces in the older brick sections.

Perhaps this house's most intriguing history is its possible association with Paul Revere. No one knows exactly where Revere was born in December 1734. Coincidentally, that year is the first possible date for this building's existence. Revere's father, Apollos Rivoire (anglicized to Paul Revere), was a goldsmith who in 1730 moved to the North End "over against C. Hutchinson's" (figure 17.2).[6] Hutchinson lived on the corner of Hanover and Fleet Streets. Since there was a church on the opposite side of Fleet Street, Revere probably lived in a house on the opposite side of Hanover Street. In 1734, the Grant House and a now demolished house stood opposite Hutchinson's house, each on opposite sides of Tileston Street where it met Hanover. It is possible that Revere Sr. moved into the "Old House" in 1730 that was torn down by Grant in 1734 and continued to live in the new building built by Grant, but the Grants appear to have also lived in the home. Either the Grants took on the Reveres as boarders, or the Reveres lived in the house on the opposite side of Tileston Street.

Today, the Grant House remains relatively unrecognized as one of the oldest buildings in Boston and the oldest on the famous Hanover Street, where it has stood for nearly three hundred years.

# 18. Faneuil Hall

Dock Square, Downtown  |  1742

Faneuil Hall is named after Peter Faneuil, who funded the construction of the 1742 building just six months before his death in 1743. Faneuil was a wealthy merchant who had made much of his fortune from the buying and selling of human beings in the Atlantic slave trade. He also inherited a considerable portion of his wealth from his fantastically wealthy uncle, Andrew, who willed the bulk of his fortune to Peter. Benjamin, Peter's brother and a potential heir to half of Andrew's wealth, was all but written out of Andrew's will when the confirmed bachelor found out that Benjamin had fallen in love. Instead, Andrew chose to give the majority of his wealth to Peter, who had followed Andrew's wishes that his heir would remain unmarried. More details on the results of this family drama can be seen with building #25, about the gatehouse of Benjamin's former estate.

Peter Faneuil's desire to fund a central market for Boston residents was controversial, with many people instead preferring the mom-and-pop push-cart vendors who populated the streets of Boston over a centralized "big box" marketplace. This issue was significant enough that several earlier central markets had been attacked and burned. With Faneuil's funding, the building of a central market became inevitable, and the town leaders selected Town Dock for its location. Town Dock was first built in 1630 and was the center of transportation and commerce for the town's import and export economy. Portions of the dock were filled in the early 1740s to create land on which to build the hall.[1]

John Smibert, a painter turned architect, designed the original brick Faneuil Hall, which was forty by a hundred feet (figure 18.1). It had Tuscan pilasters on the first floor, Doric columns on the second floor, and a full Roman Doric entablature surrounding the roofline. Smibert's original design placed the original cupola at the center of the building, giving it an overall appearance similar to that of the Old State House just down the road. The prominent tower held a grasshopper weathervane designed by Shem Drowne, who also designed the weathervane at Old North. The grasshopper contains a time capsule located in its stomach labeled "food for the grasshopper," which was added in the 1750s after the weathervane fell during a storm.[2]

FIGURE 18.1 Drawing of the original Faneuil Hall prior to its expansion in 1806 (S. Hill 1789; image courtesy of the LOC).

FIGURE 18.2
View of Faneuil
Hall in 1880, with
the elements of the
first Faneuil Hall
outlined (yellow
lines) (BPL 1880b;
image courtesy of
the BPL, edits by
author).

The first floor of the original building contained an open market with stalls
for the vendors. The second floor contained offices and a hall that could seat
a thousand people—hence, the building was named a hall, not a market. This
hall (in its various forms) was used as the primary location for Boston's town
meetings until the city was incorporated in 1822.[3]

In 1761, a fire gutted the building, and its interior was rebuilt the following year. By 1806, the building had outgrown its usefulness in its current
state, and Charles Bulfinch was employed to design its expansion. His plans
incorporated the first two stories of the southern facade of the building as
well as the first three bays of the western and eastern facades of the original
structure, but he added four new bays to the width of the structure and a
third story to the building—more than tripling the overall square footage of
the original (figure 18.2).

Significant changes to the overall structure included the relocation of the
cupola from the center of the structure to the east end of the building. Bulfinch reused many interior elements of the 1762 rebuilding to the expanded
structure, including keystones, column capitals, and doors. Much of the original purpose of the building remained, though the greatly enlarged space

included a larger public hall on the second floor and a new open space on the third floor.[4]

Significant renovations occurred throughout the nineteenth century, all done under the direction of prominent Boston architects. Alexander Parris, architect of the nearby granite Quincy Market buildings, had the building painted a grayish yellow and added a new entrance to the east facade that includes a broad staircase to the second-floor hall behind one entrance.[5]

In the second half of the nineteenth century, individual market stall renters installed canvas awnings over the entrances to their stalls from the exterior of the hall, which were later replaced by steel structures. This architectural skirt around the hall was not removed until the twentieth century.[6]

At the very end of the nineteenth century, steel beams were added to the interior columns and as much wood as possible was replaced to increase the stability of the building, with stone, steel, and iron mimicking the original wood.[7]

The twentieth century saw renovations to the interior and exterior, including the removal of several coats of paint in various colors and a significant restoration to the exterior that ended in 2019. Faneuil Hall was designated a National Historic Landmark in 1966 and a Boston Landmark in 1994. Today, the basement contains a visitor center for the National Park Service's Boston National Historical Park, the first floor is still used as merchant space, the second floor retains much of its original 1806 appearance and function as a public space for events and tours, and the third floor contains the Ancient and Honorable Society's meeting space and collections. Due to the association of the building with a prominent enslaver, it is possible that the building will be renamed.

The Shirley-Eustis House was built on a small hill overlooking the former South Bay marshes in an area that was once the rural outskirts of Roxbury (figure 19.1).

In 1746, workers began the five-year construction of William Shirley's country mansion during the first of his two terms (1741–49 and 1753–56) as governor of the Province of Massachusetts Bay.[1] In 1745, Shirley gained acclaim for capturing the Louisbourg Fortress in Nova Scotia from the French.

Shirley's new home was meant to impress, and it was likely designed by the architect Peter Harrison, who also designed King's Chapel (building #21), where Shirley worshipped. The home stands on a tall granite basement foundation, extends upward two stories, and has a partially finished attic. Its oak frame is hidden under massive two-story flattened column-like giant Doric pilasters, and wooden block-like quoins decorate the corners of the structure. A double flight of stairs on the east of the building leads upward to the bay-facing entrance under a large three-section Palladian window with a taller central arch. On the west side, a flight of stairs leads from the former carriage drive to the land-facing entrance, which is surrounded by more quoins and an oversized keystone. The original exterior boards were grooved and painted with sanded paint to resemble masonry, but around 1800 they were replaced with plain clapboards. The entire structure is capped by an ornate cupola (figure 19.2).[2]

Like the exterior, the interior was designed to impress the visitor, with an entrance featuring imported marble and a large winding staircase that leads to the second floor.[3] The east side of the house contains a two-story great hall for receptions and state banquets. In the basement, some of Shirley's enslaved people worked in the kitchen and had their living quarters.

FIGURE 19.1
A 1776 etching of Boston, showing the Shirley-Eustis House in the distance to the left (Pierrie and Newton 1776; image courtesy of the Norman B. Leventhal Map Center).

FIGURE 19.2
View of the
Shirley-Eustis
House around 1865,
before it was moved
(HNE 1865; image
courtesy of HNE).

Shirley died in the home in 1771, and it passed to his son-in-law, Eliakim Hutchinson. During the Revolution, Hutchinson abandoned the property and rebels confiscated it, using it as a hospital and barrack during the Siege of Boston.[4] After the war, the house had numerous owners, including James Magee. A captain in the China trade, Magee—with his wife, Margaret Elliot—remodeled the property in the new Federal style between 1798 and 1808, including enlarging the windows.

William Eustis, who was a surgeon during the Revolution and later twice elected governor of Massachusetts, purchased the house in 1819 and lived there with his wife, Caroline. This makes the house the only property in Massachusetts that housed both royal and elected governors. After William's death in 1825, Caroline lived a quiet life in the home and supported the abolitionist movement. Dying at the age of eighty-five in 1865, she was the longest private owner of the property.[5]

In 1867, the estate was divided into fifty-three lots and the house was divided into apartments and moved a short distance to its current location, to make room for the planned Shirley Street.[6]

The first occupants of the relocated building, the House of the Good Shepherd Catholic convent, took in so-called wayward or fallen women, including unwed mothers and prostitutes, to give them stable living space and

FIGURE 19.3
View of the east entrance of the Shirley-Eustis House, showing the Palladian window and children on the exterior staircase around 1890, when the building was home to multiple families living in apartments (HNE 1890; image courtesy of HNE).

keep them employed while living and working in the house through domestic services.[7] Approximately eighteen women at a time lived in the house, half of them nuns and the other half reforming "Magdalenes," before the organization moved to a new, larger building in Mission Hill in 1871. A clergyman lived alone in the house for the rest of the 1870s.

In the early 1880s, individual renters arrived, and multiple working-class families occupied the house (figure 19.3). The 1880 census shows most of the home's residents had been born in various New England states, while others had been born in Russia, Baden-Baden (Germany), Sweden, and Ireland. By 1900, most of the families living in the home had been born in Massachusetts or Canada and were primarily of Irish ancestry. These families had probably moved to Roxbury as industrial jobs appeared in the surrounding area.

When the Shirley-Eustis House Association was formed and purchased the house in 1913,[8] many of the original interior architectural elements that had been removed where found in storage spaces in the house or in the private home of an architect in Back Bay. These elements have been carefully restored, and others have been re-created. Though the building is a National Historic Landmark, it is not a Boston Landmark. The Shirley-Eustis House and property is maintained as a historic house museum, with tours provided during most of the year.

# 20. Thomas Gardner House

26–28 Higgins Street, Allston-Brighton  |  Ca. 1747

In 1747, Richard Gardner purchased 110 acres at the corner of Harvard and Brighton Avenues and paid workers to build a gambrel-roofed house three bays wide by two bays deep for himself; his wife, Elizabeth; and their son, Thomas. Thomas would inherit the home and live there with his wife, Joanna Sparhawk—who came from a prominent founding family of Little Cambridge, as the Allston-Brighton neighborhood was originally named.[1]

The house was big for both the region and the time, and its size reflects the wealth and significance of the Gardners. Thomas Gardner was born in 1724 and served as a selectman and representative to the General Court, which met in the Old State House (see building #7). He was an active participant in the events that led up to the Revolution. After the 1773 Boston Tea Party, King George III dissolved the General Court, and Gardner became an outspoken opponent of the royal actions. He was selected to represent Cambridge in both the Middlesex County Convention and the Provincial Congress. This congress served the legal needs of those who sided with the rebels during the Revolution and became the seat of government after the war. It eventually would form a constitutional convention, which adopted the Massachusetts Constitution.[2]

In addition to his political role, Gardner played a major military role in the region. He was elected to the rank of colonel and, having organized a regiment himself, led it during the Battle of Bunker Hill on June 17, 1775. Gardner was mortally wounded during the fight, but he did not die until July 3. In recognition of his actions, George Washington attended his funeral, and the town of Gardner, Massachusetts, was named in his honor.[3]

In the mid-nineteenth century, increasing demand for commercial structures in the growing Allston area of Allston-Brighton, and the construction of larger Victorian mansions resulted in the demolition of many earlier homes in the formerly dense residential area around the Gardner House. Fortunately, the house was moved to a residential block on Higgins Street and continued to house members of the rapidly growing population of Allston (figures 20.1 and 20.2). Today, the building has two paired interior chimneys, which probably replaced an original large central chimney that would have served

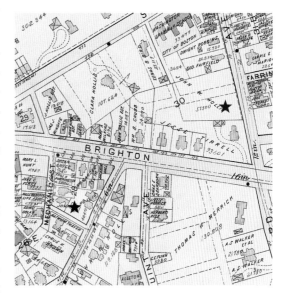

FIGURE 20.1
An 1899 map of Allston showing the original location of the Thomas Gardner House (the red star in the upper right) and its current location (the black star in the lower left) (Richards 1899; image courtesy of the Norman B. Leventhal Map Center).

the fireplaces in every room of the house. The two chimneys were probably added when the building was converted to apartments.

Earlier windows and clapboards recorded in the 1970s have been replaced by newer vinyl windows and exterior siding. Additions include a shed roof to the east; a two-story wing with a broad gable roof to the west; an enclosed addition to the main entrance; and two-story polygonal bay windows added to the west of the entrance in a style similar to that of the Ebenezer Smith House (see building #10), also located in Allston-Brighton. The Gardner House does not have Boston Landmark status or state or federal historic designation.

# 21. King's Chapel

58 Tremont Street, Downtown | 1750

Anglicans were unpopular among Boston's predominantly Congregationalist (Puritan) residents, so the first King's Chapel, a 1688 wooden structure, was built in an undignified corner of the town's first cemetery, now King's Chapel Burying Ground (figure 21.1). While the church is located immediately adjacent to the burying ground that shares its name, the two have always functioned independently of each other.

The original wood church was expanded in 1710. However, it soon outgrew its footprint, requiring the purchase of land from the town of Boston—which owned the surrounding cemetery and the nearby Boston Latin School, on the north side of School Street.[1] To accommodate the church's expansion, the school would have to be torn down. There was great outcry by Bostonians over the planned demolition, which triggered an early discussion in Boston about the separation of church and state. One resident, John Green, Esq., wrote:

A fig for your learning! I tell you the Town,
To make the church larger, must pull the school down.
Unluckily spoken, replied Master Birch,
Then learning, I fear, stops the growth of the church.[2]

FIGURE 21.1
Drawing of an approximation of the appearance of the original King's Chapel (Stark 1901; image courtesy of the BPL).

The expansion plans were ultimately successful, and the congregation purchased a plot of land across the street for the new building of the Latin School.

The new church was designed by Peter Harrison, who probably also designed the Shirley-Eustis House (see building #19).[3] His designs called for the use of Quincy granite for the exterior walls. Stone buildings were rare in Boston and included the Hancock Manor (discussed in the introduction) and the nearby Cooke Mansion (located directly behind King's Chapel, on School Street). Both mansions were standing when King's Chapel was constructed but have since been demolished.

Because there were no alternative places for the congregation to worship, the current church was built around the original wooden structure, which was dismantled after the stone church was completed.[4]

The original plans included a stone spire, but funding shortages resulted in the boxy front tower that remains unfinished today.

Very little of the 1750 interior has been changed, excluding the paint—which would have been darker and more colorful, including pink and peach tones, than the present mostly white interior. Still, the building remains

one of the finest and most intact examples of Georgian church architecture in the country (figure 21.2). The pulpit is one of the few interior elements from the original wooden building and dates to 1718, soon after an expansion of the original structure.

The exterior features several wooden elements, including the massive Doric columns, trim, and wooden balustrade. All are painted a grayish brown in imitation of sandstone.[5]

During the Revolution, the church sat vacant. In 785, it became the first Episcopal church in the western hemisphere to convert to Unitariansm, and it remains Unitarian today. At present, the church has an active congregation with regular services and sermons. Though it is a National Historic Landmark, it is not a Boston Landmark. The building is open daily for tours of its interior and crypt, and it regularly hosts concerts, other performances, and community events.

FIGURE 21.2
The interior of King's Chapel in the late nineteenth century (BPL 1880c; image courtesy of the BPL).

The Dillaway-Thomas House, Roxbury First Church, and the nearby Spooner-Lambert House (see building #32) constitute a group of well-preserved early buildings near Roxbury's historic town center.

In 1752, the Reverend Oliver Peabody, pastor of the First Church, declared his intentions to begin building "a beautiful house on the north side of Eliot Square," across the road from the church.[1] Sadly, he died just weeks later, and it appears that William Peabody, a later pastor, began construction on the house in the same year. A 1754 deed describes the building as partially finished, and a later owner, the Reverend Amos Adams, lamented in a 1762 letter that though he lived in it, the house remained "unfinished" and "unadorned."[2]

The long-delayed completion can be blamed on a combination of the First Church's lack of provision for funding the building of a parsonage and the relatively poor pay of early ministers in the church, despite the overall wealth of colonial Roxbury residents. Stylistically, the building—five by two bays, with a gambrel roof—is a large mid-eighteenth-century Georgian home, constructed on a scale that was quite expensive when you consider that the building was intended to be an unofficial home for a poorly paid religious leader.

Though the Dillaway-Thomas House functioned as a parsonage, the church never owned the house, nor was it provided for the pastor. Still, for much of its first hundred years, it was owned by pastors.

During the Revolution, rebel forces constructed a series of earthworks and temporary fortifications in the immediate vicinity of the Dillaway-Thomas House and First Church. John Thomas, a rebel general, commandeered the house from the church for use as officer housing. The property's location along a ridge facing Boston, today obscured by trees, allowed for an unbroken view across the neck of Boston to Charlestown, and it is said that Thomas watched Charlestown burn from the upper windows of the house during the Battle of Bunker Hill, on June 17, 1775.[3] The house remained relatively intact throughout the Revolution, and after the death of Amos Adams in 1775, the property was sold to the Reverend Eliphalet Porter, who lived in the house until his death in 1833. Porter was a major figure in local organizations, but he took in boarders, probably to supplement his income as the pastor at First Church and to offset the costs of maintaining the large home.[4]

When Porter died, ownership of the house passed on to his niece, Martha Ruggles Porter. Martha had married Charles K. Dillaway, a teacher at and headmaster of the Boston Latin School and a trustee of the Roxbury Latin School. His primary passion was education and the classics, but he was also involved with the First Church, serving as deacon and superintendent of the church's Sunday school.

In the late nineteenth century, the house played a major role in early US-Japanese relations. After 220 years of an isolationist foreign policy called *sokoku*, or "closed country," Japan admitted trade soon after the signing of the 1858 Treaty of Amity and Commerce with the United States, also known as the Harris Treaty.[5] In 1870, the Boston merchant Aaron Davis Weld French was visited by four young Japanese men who had come to study in the United States. Dillaway, a noted teacher and an associate of French through the Boston and Roxbury Latin Schools, taught the four Japanese students in the Dillaway-Thomas House in one of the first Japanese-American cultural exchanges (figure 22.1).[6]

Dillaway passed away in 1889, but his wife, Martha, remained in the relatively unchanged house until her death in 1903. It then had a series of owners before the City of Boston purchased the building in 1927, to demolish it for the construction of the adjacent Timilty School.[7]

The Roxbury Historical Society fought the demolition and succeeded in getting a bill passed in the state legislature in 1930 that protected the house and provided $25,000 toward its restoration. The architect Frank Chouteau Brown undertook the restoration. In the 1930s, the society occupied portions of the building, paying a nominal fee to the city. In the 1970s, a series of arson events damaged but did not destroy the building. In 1984, community

FIGURE 22.1
Portrait of Charles Dillaway with the four Japanese students, Hanabusa Kotarô, Hiraga Isosaburô, Tsuge Zengo, and Aoki Yoshihira, Sonrel 1870; image courtesy of the Museum of Fine Arts, Boston).

FIGURE 22.2 Byron Rushing in front of the Dillaway-Thomas House as it appeared in 1981, after a fire and general decay. Rushing, a member of the Massachusetts House of Representatives in 1983–2019, was a key figure in the house's protection and restoration soon after this photo was taken and in more recent times (BLC 1981; image courtesy of the City of Boston Archives).

activists—including the Roxbury Historical Society and Byron Rushing, then a state representative—raised funds to restore the house as part of the Roxbury Heritage State Park created under Michael Dukakis, then governor of Massachusetts (figure 22.2).[8] The house reopened in 1992 with exhibits on Roxbury's history and the construction phases of the house.

In 2014, Governor Deval Patrick authorized funds to restore the house and nearby park. After this state-funded restoration effort to reinterpret the interior of the building as a Roxbury history museum and community space, the house reopened in 2019 with multiple new exhibitions. The property is listed on the National Register and is part of a group of buildings in the Roxbury Highlands area waiting for a Study Report as part of the process of becoming a Boston Landmark.

# 23. Linden Hall

26–28 Grovenor Road, Jamaica Plain │ 1755

In 1755, the merchant John Gould paid for the construction of a large home for his daughter, Sarah, and her future husband, the Reverend John Troutbeck, on a large parcel on Center Street.[1] Troutbeck was the assistant rector of King's Chapel (see building #21)[2] and a distiller, a profession frowned upon by some members of the community, including the author of the following poem:

> John, of small merit, who deals in the spirit,
> As next in course I sing;
> Fain would I treat, as is most meet,
> This chaplain of the King.
> His Sunday aim is to reclaim
> Those that in vice are sunk;
> When Monday's come, he selleth rum,
> And gets them plaguey drunk.[3]

Like many buildings in this book, Troutbeck's home was moved to save it from demolition. It once stood near the southwest corner of Centre and Pond Streets, with grounds extending far back to Jamaica Pond. In its original setting, the house had a hipped roof and end chimneys, with two large wings on either side creating a monumental structure. The estate featured an expansive lawn down to Jamaica Pond and was known to have large linden trees along the walk to its entrance, giving it the name Linden Hall.[4]

FIGURE 23.1
A late-nineteenth-century view of Linden Hall with its original wings, prior to its move (BLC 1875; image courtesy of the City of Boston Archives).

FIGURE 23.2 Aerial drawing of Jamaica Plain showing Jamaica Pond (in the distance), Linden Hall in its original location (the lower red star) and its current location (the upper white star) (O. H. Bailey and Co. 1891; image courtesy of the Norman B. Leventhal Map Center, edits by author).

Jamaica Pond is one of the few natural ponds in Boston. Its size, coupled with its ideal distance from Boston (not too close, not too far), provided an ideal setting for wealthy residents to build large estates along its shores. Though the individual properties have shrunk in size over the years, some of the largest homes in Boston can still be found around Jamaica Pond.

In 1776, Troutbeck and his wife, both Tories, abandoned the property and fled Boston.[5] After the Revolution, a third story was added to the building, and it was converted into Charles W. Greene's Academy, a college preparatory school for boys (figure 23.1).[6] In 1840, a dancing school was established in the building, which indicates the overall scale of the rooms inside the mansion.[7]

The city laid out Grovenor Road in 1890 just behind Linden Hall, and between 1896 and 1905 the mansion was moved to make way for structures built closer to the street (figure 23.2). After the move, Linden Hall was converted into apartments.[8]

The house is not a city Landmark, but it is listed on the National Register as a contributing property to the Monument Square Historic District. Though the interior of the structure has been broken up, the windows replaced, and vinyl siding added, this property is one of the few surviving grand early homes around Jamaica Pond. Importantly, Linden Hall is not a museum, but it remains a home to Bostonians—the purpose for which it was originally built.

# 24. Loring Greenough House

12 South Street, Jamaica Plain  |  1760

Unlike Linden Hall, located just down the road, this stately home retains not only its overall historic appearance but also some of its original setting.

The home was built for Commodore Joshua Loring, a commander of the English forces on the Great Lakes during the Seven Years' War.[1] After a distinguished military career, he chose to retire to a farm in West Roxbury, now Jamaica Plain. He purchased the farm estate in 1752, had the Third Church parsonage that stood there removed (see the Honorable Mentions), and had workers begin construction of a large home.[2]

Loring's house is a tall, square building, with two and a half stories, five bays on each side, and a Georgian-style hipped roof. The Chinese Chippendale–style latticework railing along the roofline is original and reflects the owner's high-end design tastes (figure 24.1).[3]

The house's two original eighteenth-century doors would have been located on the north (garden) and south (parking area) sides of the home. Each are massive twelve-panel doors, meaning there are twelve flat areas within the design of the door, making them extremely wide and grand—as well as typical of elite homes in the Georgian period. The north door was moved to the newer west-side entrance facing Centre Street and replaced with a smaller Federal-style door in the nineteenth century, using sidelight windows to fill in the gap to either side of the smaller door.[4]

The carriage house connected to the east of the mansion, which also contains the last existing summer kitchen in Boston, was built in 1811, and the original gardens and immediate surroundings remain (figure 24.2). Earlier maps indicate that there were multiple outbuildings, including a barn to the east of the house, which have been lost to development. Though much of the original estate has been developed, the house remains inside a relatively large parcel, which helps maintain its overall appearance as a grand Georgian home in a rural setting—much as it was in the eighteenth century.[5]

Loring and his family were Tories and fled during the Revolution. For four weeks starting on June 3, 1775, the rebel General Nathanael Greene used the house as his headquarters and a hospital for people wounded during fighting nearby. As a result, the property has been designated a National Medical Landmark by the American Association for the History of Medicine. The dead were buried nearby on an area of the once large estate but were later exhumed and moved to Peter's Hill cemetery, now in the Arnold Arboretum.[6]

In 1783, the Commonwealth of Massachusetts sold the house to Anne Doane, a widow and wealthy heiress. She married David Stoddard Greenough, a society lawyer who had represented her late husband, three months later, and their family remained in the home for five generations. In 1907, the house

FIGURE 24.2
Plan drawing of the Loring Greenough estate in 1937, showing the main building, landscaping, and outbuildings at the time (M. Webster 1937; image courtesy of the Historic American Buildings Survey).

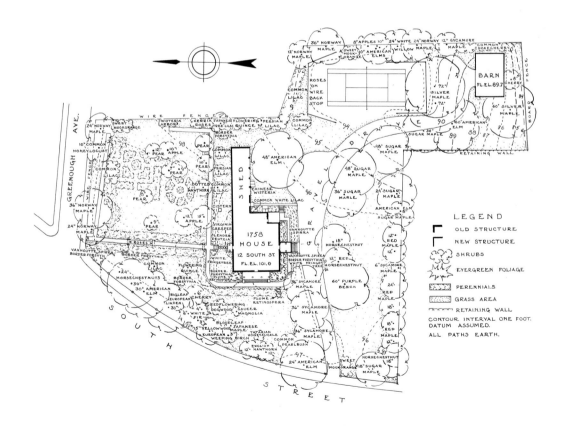

was modernized, adding plumbing and new floors to portions of the building before the family put the house on the market in 1924.[7]

Meanwhile, the Jamaica Plain Tuesday Club, a women's organization, was formed in 1896.[8] (In the nineteenth century, there were popular men's clubs in Boston named for every evening in the week, except for Tuesday and Sunday.) Design plans for a row of three-deckers and stores on the house's property were already in existence when the Tuesday Club decided to purchase it from a group of developers and convert the house into its headquarters (figure 24.3). To partially finance the maintenance of the house, it sold off portions of the land south of the house in the 1950s.[9]

The Loring Greenough House remains owned and operated by the Jamaica Plain Tuesday Club, which recently dropped the hyphen in the house's official name (originally it was known as the Loring-Greenough House). In 1999, the house, its interior, and surrounding lands were collectively designated a Boston Landmark. The property, listed on the National Register, is used for public and private community events—including weddings, lectures, movies, and other gatherings—for the diverse and vibrant Jamaica Plain community.

FIGURE 25.1

View of the Faneuil
estate prior to the
fire that destroyed
the mansion house
(the red arrow in
the center), show-
ing the Faneuil
gatehouse (the
black arrow on
the right) (Brigh-
ton-Allston Histor-
ical Society 1900a;
image courtesy of
the society).

This small gambrel-roofed house is all that remains of the massive seventy-
acre estate of Benjamin Faneuil, brother of the infamous Peter Faneuil (see
building #18). Benjamin and Peter were sons of French-born Huguenots
who joined their wildly wealthy uncle, Andrew Faneuil, in Boston after their
father's death.

Andrew, a confirmed bachelor, offered to include both brothers in his will
if they remained single. When Benjamin fell in love with his future wife,
Mary, he was cut out of his uncle's life and fled to Europe. While Peter grew
wealthy as a well-connected slave trader, Benjamin followed a quieter path.
In his will, Andrew left the vast majority of his wealth and estate to Peter,
leaving Benjamin just "five shillings and no more."[1]

After Andrew's death in 1738, Peter became the wealthiest man in Boston.
Just six years later, Peter died without a will. Because he was an unmarried
man, the majority of his estate went to Benjamin, who then had the combined
fortunes of Andrew and Peter—the largest inheritance in Boston's history.
Included in Peter's estate were five enslaved people (their ages and genders
were not recorded). It is likely that Benjamin became the enslaver of these
people, but it is not known if they lived in Brighton.[2]

Benjamin Faneuil continued his quiet life, purchasing seventy acres for a
new family home in the Brighton area of what is now the Allston-Brighton
neighborhood in 1761.[3] After having an older building demolished, he funded
the construction of a massive mansion and many outbuildings—presumably

including the gatehouse that still stands, though there are few detailed records of the function of the buildings on the property other than the main
mansion (figure 25.1).

As the wealthiest man in the region, Faneuil was able to garnish his house
in the most expensive means available. One particularly notable aspect of his
home was his parlor, whose walls were lined with wood paneling. Each board
was fifty-two inches wide.[4]

Benjamin Fanueil moved to Brighton with Mary, his wife; and their three
children, Benjamin, Peter, and Mary. Benjamin Faneuil Sr. would spend the
remainder of his life in Brighton, but he experienced some turmoil in his
later years.[5]

It is said that on behalf of Benjamin Sr.'s daughter, Mary, her manservant—who may have lived in the gatekeeper house and may have been one
of Peter Faneuil's enslaved men—invited General George Washington when
he passed by to enter the house. There, Mary invited Washington to return
with General Charles Lee for dinner. Her Tory father, now blind and senile,
unknowingly dined with the men. When he was informed of the identity
of his guests, he complimented Washington as a leader but accused Lee of
treason. Mary apologized to Washington and Lee, and it may have been her

FIGURE 25.2
View of the gate-
house around 1920,
after the loss of the
main Faneuil man-
sion (Brighton-
Allston Historical
Society 1920; image
courtesy of the
society).

apology that allowed the property to remain in her family's ownership during and after the Revolution—despite its association with Tories.[6]

When Benjamin Sr. died in 1786, he left the estate to his daughter and her husband, George Bethune. The property would remain in the ownership of several wealthy Brighton families until the mansion burned in 1917, and the gatehouse became a separate property (figure 25.2). In 1924, the Crittenton Women's Union (recently renamed EMPath) built a large building in the rear of the Faneuil estate, and that remains owned by the organization. The owners play a valuable role in providing services for low-income people trying to reach economic independence.

Though the gatekeeper house has had a lean-to added to its back and a porch to the front, this early piece of Brighton history retains its overall small scale and eighteenth-century form. In the late 1990s, Brighton residents submitted a petition to the Boston Landmarks Commission, seeking to make the building a Boston Landmark. The property is a pending Landmark, as a Study Report is still required. It has no other historic designations or recognitions.

# 26. Gardiner Building

60 Long Wharf, Downtown | 1763

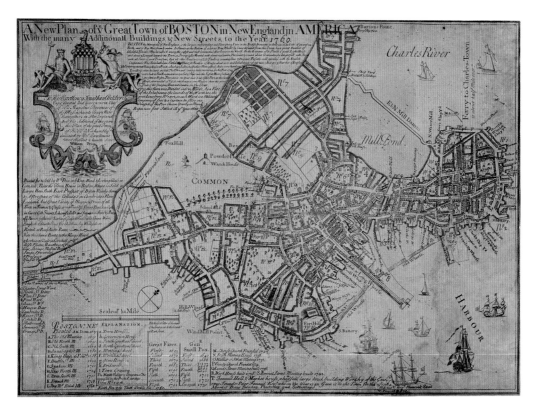

FIGURE 26.
William Price's 1769
map of Boston,
based on John
Bonner's map from
the early eighteenth
century, showing
Long Wharf (lower
right) extending
dramatically into
Boston Harbor
(Price and Bonner
1769; image courtesy
of the Norman B.
Leventhal Map
Center).

Boston's original 1630 Town Dock was located where Faneuil Hall (see building #18) is today and was surrounded by many other wharves (the structures) and docks (the water next to the structures) along Boston's shore. By the beginning of the eighteenth century, the existing wharves were not sufficient to meet the needs of a growing city, so merchants and investors proposed a new massive wharf.

In 1710, the Proprietors of Long Wharf, headed by Captain Oliver Noyes, successfully convinced the selectmen of Boston to build Long Wharf.[1]

The wharf was designed to extend from King Street over mudflats that would be exposed at low tide, pass the Barricado, a massive defensive wood and stone wall encircling Boston's port, and go an additional 200 feet beyond it (figure 26.1). The wharf would include a thirty-foot-wide street on the south side, buildings along the north side, and another four feet of walkway behind the buildings. The wharf extended over a half-mile out of Boston, and its length was divided into seventy-one building lots for warehouses and stores numbered from west to east. The larger lots to the west measured forty feet wide and twenty feet deep, with the eastern ones measuring twenty-four and a half feet by twenty feet.[2] The structure on lot 60 is the oldest remaining and one of the oldest buildings in Boston.

Building on the wharf began rapidly, with many lots filled by the early eighteenth century. Long Wharf was and still is a site of mercantilism and a public space where merchants could import and store goods and the general public could shop.

The building on lot 60 was built in 1763 and owned by Giles Alexander, the clerk and agent for the Proprietors of Long Wharf.[3] This lot consists of the eastern twenty-four and a half feet of the existing Gardner Building and is most visible as the span between the two chimneys on the eastern end of the building (figure 26.2). Originally, there would have been two additional buildings extending to the ocean on the eastern side of lot 60 and just one building on the left of twenty-four and a half feet.

The building would have served as a storage warehouse for goods unloaded from nearby ships. During the Revolution, this building witnessed the arrival of British troops during the Siege of Boston; their flight during Evacuation Day, on March 16, 1776; and the arrival of Massachusetts's copy of the Declaration of Independence four months later (figure 26.3).

In 1807, Alexander sold the building to Samuel Hammond, a merchant, who retained ownership until the 1850s.[4] The remaining portion of the brick building to the west was added in 1830, and this probably coincided with significant updating of the older eastern portion of the building.[5] After Hammond's death, the property was owned by successive trustees of his estate, including Robert H. Gardiner (hence the building's name), until the 1920s.[6] Throughout much of this time, the both the property and most of the other

FIGURE 26.2
Approximate location of the former edge of the Gardner Building (yellow line; photo and edits by author).

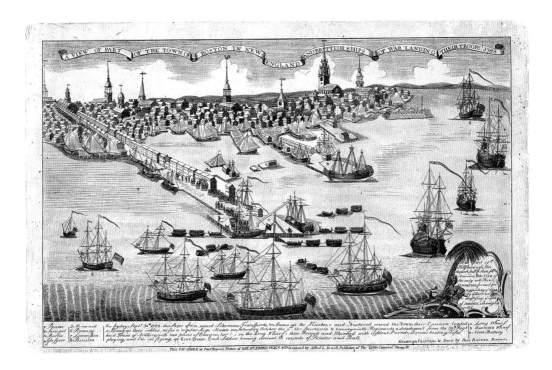

A VIEW OF PART OF THE TOWN OF BOSTON IN NEW ENGLAND AND BRITISH SHIPS OF WAR LANDING THEIR TROOPS 1768

FIGURE 26.3
Paul Revere's
1768 view of Long
Wharf, showing
British ships un-
loading troops
during the Siege
of Boston (Revere
1768; image cour-
tesy of the Norman
B. Leventhal Map
Center).

buildings on Long Wharf remained warehouses and served the needs of merchants and retailers there.

During the nineteenth century, Boston slowly regained its commercial identity as it recovered from the devastating War of 1812, which peaked in its commercial success as a mercantile leader in the 1840s. The arrival of freight trains that would have a great impact Boston's role as a trade powerhouse. Ironically, the first train to arrive in America was unloaded from a ship at Long Wharf in 1830. Boston's marine industry and the significance of Long Wharf declined, but the Gardiner Building and the neighboring Custom House Block to the east remained in commercial use throughout most of the twentieth century.

In 1973, the Gardiner Building was rehabilitated, with major changes to its interior. It was then converted into a restaurant and remains so today, most recently housing a restaurant in the Chart House chain.[7] Today, the building is a National Historic Landmark but not a Boston Landmark.

# 27. Ebenezer Hancock House

10 Marshall Street, Downtown | 1767

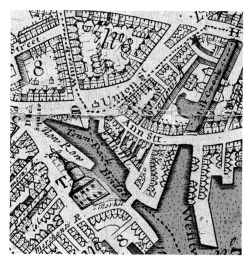

FIGURE 27.1 Detailed view of the 1769 Price and Bonner map of Boston (see figure 26.1), showing bodies of water (blue) near the Ebenezer Hancock House (the red star in the upper right): Town Dock (lower left), Mill Creek (upper right), and Scottow's Dock (the small bay on Mill Creek) (Price 1769; image courtesy of the Norman B. Leventhal Map Center, edits by author).

When Europeans first arrived in Boston in the early 1600s, what would become the North End neighborhood was nearly detached from the main portion of Boston by a narrow, brackish stream that ran between the former Town Dock and Mill Pond. To reach the North End on North Street, near Faneuil Hall (see building #18), one would need to cross a toll bridge over Mill Creek. By the late seventeenth century, this area had been developed by merchants and others whose access to the creek and Scottow's Dock allowed them to ship their goods in and out of Boston via boat (figure 27.1). To build in the area, which included the future site of the Ebenezer Hancock House, the shallow marshy land required filling and wharfing out—the process of building a wharf, filling in the dock next to it, and repeating the process.

FIGURE 27.2 View of the corner of the Ebenezer Hancock House around 1898 (BPL 1898b; image courtesy of the BPL).

In 1763, John Hancock inherited a parcel of land on Marshall Street from his uncle. In 1767, he purchased additional land on the street and began construction of a home that would soon be occupied by his brother, Ebenezer Hancock.[1]

The house is a modest three-story home with Flemish bond brickwork (alternating narrow and wide brick sides in each row), the almost obligatory eighteenth-century belt courses, three chimneys, and a rear ell (figure 27.2). The fifth window bay at the corner of the house is canted to better fit the original seventeenth-century street layout and parcel shape. On the exterior, the brickwork, windows, early shutters, some hinges, and much of the window hardware are original.

The house has one of the best preserved early interiors in Boston. On the first floor, original and early elements include paneling in the hallway of the staircase, window details (excluding the storefront), wooden chimney supports, nineteenth-century built-in shelving, and the original fireplace with beehive ovens. Two of the second-story rooms have intact mantelpieces with end panels, and the third floor has original plaster and lath ceilings with period hand-wrought nails (figure 27.3). Both of the upper floors retain much of their original door hardware, floors, woodwork, and original room size and layout.[2]

FIGURE 27.3
A 1934 image of the interior decorative elements on the second floor of the Ebenezer Hancock House, one of several images of the interior taken during documentation for the Historic American Buildings Survey (Haskell 1934; image courtesy of the survey).

The house served as the Continental Army paymaster's headquarters during the lead-up to the Revolution. Ebenezer Hancock was a deputy paymaster general of the army—which developed in 1775 from all thirteen American colonies that would fight the British regulars. There are reports that two million French silver crowns from King Louis xvi were stored in the home—a loan for financing the army that Benjamin Franklin had negotiated while in Paris in 1778.[3]

The house was sold in the 1780s, first becoming the glass and ceramic store of Ebenezer Frothingham. In 1798, it was sold to Benjamin Fuller, a shoe dealer, beginning a tradition of having shoe merchants in the first-floor storefronts that lasted nearly two centuries, until 1969.[4]

To satisfy the needs of merchants in the late eighteenth century, the large storefront windows were added to the first floor, and a second narrow entrance was added between the two first-floor stores.[5]

The house is greatly enhanced by the original seventeenth-century street layout and surrounding early buildings in the Blackstone Block where it resides. Today, it is occupied by Schwartz and Schwartz, a legal firm that purchased the property after it was left vacant following a serious car accident in the 1970s, which nearly destroyed the storefront at the corner of the building. The firm has sensitively restored the building and its interior to its nineteenth-century appearance, retaining its remaining eighteenth-century components.[6]

The Ebenezer Hancock House remains the only house in Boston's downtown built during the Revolution. In recognition of its historic significance and remarkably intact interior, the house is listed on the National Register and was designated a Boston Landmark in 1978 for both its exterior and interior architectural features.

# 28. Charles Tileston House

13 River Street, Dorchester  |  Ca. 1770

FIGURE 28.1
Aerial view of
Lower Mills at the
southern end of
Dorchester, show-
ing the location of
the Tileston House
(red star) relative
to other buildings
in the village center
(O. H. Bailey and
Co. 1890b; image
courtesy of the
Norman B. Leven-
thal Map Center,
edits by author).

The Charles Tileston House is the oldest building in Lower Mills, having been built around 1770. It is a tall, gambrel-roofed house with symmetrical five-bay front and two bays on its side. The surrounding area has been a center of mill industries since the 1630s, due to the Neponset River rapids that cascade over the pudding-stone bedrock on the border between Dorchester and Milton (figure 28.1). These mills brought with them both the industry of grist, wood, and paper mills and the homes of associated workers and craftspeople.

In the 1740s, Edward Capen began purchasing dozens of acres of land along the road to Dedham, as River Street was then known, just west of the mills. Edward's daughter, Patience, married Ezra Badlam, and the house passed to them after Edward's death in 1770.[1] Ezra and Patience lived in the house, and Ezra probably ran his furniture-making business in the nearby shop on the same property (now demolished) with his brother Stephen, who lived across the street.

The brothers are both significant historical figures in American military and art history. Colonel Ezra Badlam and Sergeant Stephen Badlam fought in the Massachusetts Militia and Continental Army during the Revolution.[2] Prior to the war, in the early 1770s, Ezra taught Stephen the cabinet-making trade. Stephen's work was exceptional and can be found in collections at Yale University and the Metropolitan Museum of Art (figure 28.2).

No surviving example of Ezra's work has been identified, but his 1788 probate inventory includes over four thousand linear feet of mahogany, maple, wide pine, narrow pine, cherry, and ash.³ Before his death, Ezra sold multiple properties that he had either purchased or inherited through his wife, including the George Haynes House (see building #37).

In 1788, Ezra sold half ownerships of the Charles Tileston House to Richard Trow and Euclid Tileston, including an adjacent carriage shop.⁴ Trow and Tileston were employees of Ezra, and they each married one of Ezra's daughters after buying the house together.

According to the 1800 census, Tileston, then married to Hannah Badlam, lived in the house with Hannah's mother, Patience; Hannah's four youngest siblings; and their own four children.⁵ Hannah died in 1801. Three years later, Tileston married Jane Withington and had four more children.

When Tileston died in 1848, the property was divided among his and Hannah's children, but one of the heirs—Charles Tileston—bought out his siblings and became the sole owner in 1849. Because his name appeared on the earliest map of the area with named properties in 1850, it has been associated with the house in official building surveys.⁶ Charles was a businessman and owned a store that sold stoves and tin goods next door, at the intersection of River and Washington Streets. After Charles's death in 1894, the property had multiple owners—often people who also owned shops in Lower Mills (figure 28.3).

Today, the house has no state or federal historic designations. Though it retains its overall shape and size, all its windows have been replaced, it is

FIGURE 28.2 *left* A chest-on-chest made by Stephen Badlam in 1791 (Yale University 2010; image courtesy of Yale University Art Gallery).

FIGURE 28.3 *right* Photo of the Tileston House around 1890 (DHS 1890c; image courtesy of the DHS).

currently covered in mint-green vinyl siding, its front door has been replaced, it has lost its Victorian porch, and it has gutters for window boxes.

The property was recently purchased to demolish it for an entrance to a nearby parking lot. The Dorchester Historical Society filed a petition for the house to receive Boston Landmark status and stop the demolition, and the demolition plans were soon dropped. The house was sold again, and the new owners plan to renovate it. After detailed ownership research by Kathleen von Jena—the assistant survey director of the BLC—in December 2019, the BLC voted to accept the Landmark petition, and the Tileston House became a pending Boston Landmark.

# 29. Joseph Royall House

770 Washington Street, Dorchester | Ca. 1770

In 1737, Isaac Royall purchased five hundred acres in Medford, Massachusetts, and set about expanding an earlier building into a large family home and nearby housing for at least twenty-seven enslaved men, women, and children that he brought with his family from Antigua.[1] This house, now known as the Royall House and Slave Quarters, serves as one of the most significant house museums in New England, as it includes the only remaining slave quarters in the region and plays an important role in the increasing examination and uncovering of the story of slavery in the North.

Isaac's children who survived him included Isaac Jr., who inherited his father's massive estate, and Penelope, who married Henry Vassal in 1742. After squandering both his and her inheritances, Henry Vassal died in 1769, leaving Penelope their large estate in Cambridge. Penelope and Isaac Jr.'s paternal cousin, also named Isaac, was born in Dorchester and had two sons. One of them, Robert, was a housewright and helped build the third church on Meeting House Hill in 1743.[2] Robert's son, Joseph Royall, also lived in Dorchester, but he appears infrequently in historic records.

Around 1770, Joseph Royall paid for the construction of a house at what is now the corner of Washington and Ashmont Streets. At the time, this was open land to the east of the main road from Dorchester to Boston. There are no records of Joseph buying or inheriting the land, so a more precise date for construction is not possible through historic records, and its general construction style is the best evidence available.

The house is a broad and low Georgian, with a five-bay front facade, an L-shape addition on the north side of the house, and early decorative columns on either side of the original eighteenth-century front door.

When the Revolution broke out, the Tory Royalls were forced to flee. Isaac Jr. went to Nova Scotia and ended up in England.[3] Joseph ended up in London, and Penelope abandoned her Cambridge property and fled to Antigua with her daughter, Elizabeth.[4] After the war, Isaac Jr. and Joseph remained in England, but Penelope returned to Boston.

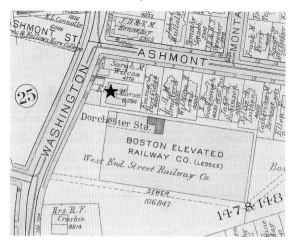

FIGURE 29.1 A map in a 1918 atlas, showing the nearby elevated railroad structures where the YMCA is currently located, as well as buildings in front of the Royall House (the red star) (G. W. Bromley and Co. 1918; image courtesy of the Norman B. Leventhal Map Center, edits by author).

FIGURE 29.2 Images of the Joseph Royall House during renovations in the 1980s, including the demolition of the one-story commercial buildings in the front (Rugo 1985; images courtesy of Bob Rugo).

Because her husband had lost most of their fortune before he died and her Cambridge home had been seized, she was destitute.

It appears that Joseph, Penelope's first cousin twice removed, had quite a bit of sympathy for his relative back in Boston. In 1782, he sold her his Dorchester house and land as well as an additional property in Milton—amounting to thirty acres in all—for just five shillings.[5] Penelope's desperation is made clear by the fact that the very next deed in the records for 1782 is her sale of the same property to Desire Toleman and his wife, Sarah Howe, of Dorchester for 141 pounds sterling.[6]

The Tolemans sold the property two years later to Samuel Pierce, who is probably the Colonel Samuel Pierce Jr. of the Pierce House (see building #3) and who probably used it as a rental property.[7] In 1796, Abraham Pierce, a leather tanner, and his wife, Lois, purchased the property from Samuel,

Abraham's father.[8] When Abraham and Lois sold the property in 1811, it was still a multi-acre parcel with a house near the road, and it remained so until the end of the nineteenth century.[9] After Charles Dodge purchased the property in 1867,[10] he began to sell off the lots along Ashmont Street. A building boom in the late Victorian neighborhood of Ashmont Hill was then beginning, spurred on by Boston's annexation of Dorchester, the arrival of the street car, and a new street grid in the area.

The newer homes along the northern end of the property still left a large area of open land to the south of the Royall House. By 1904, the Boston Elevated Railway had built its Dorchester Station (which was later replaced with the Dorchester YMCA) just feet from the home's southern edge (figure 29.1).[11] Taking advantage of the major commercial activities occurring along the entire length of Washington Street, two small one-story wooden shops were added in the front yard of the house around 1899. However, they did not touch the historic house behind them, preserving the building's original front facade.

In 1981, Ashmont Hill neighbors Bob Rugo and Michael Stella purchased the house, aided by loans from other neighbors, removed the storefronts, and restored the historic home (figure 29.2). Michael still owns the house as rental property. It has no state or federal historic designations and is not a designated Boston Landmark.

# 30. Clap-Field House

1444 Dorchester Avenue, Dorchester  |  Ca. 1772

Though this is hard to tell today, the Clap-Field House traces its history back to one of the more prolific Dorchester families, which owned multiple properties listed in this book. The Clap family settled first in the northern end of Dorchester (for more of its early history, see building #4). By the end of the eighteenth century, Clap descendants could be found throughout Dorchester. One enclave of Claps or Clapps (different family members preferred different spellings) was near what would become known as Fields Corner.

Like most seventeenth-century streets in Boston, Adams Street likely began its history as a Massachusett Native trail that followed the transition between higher, dry land and the marshy lands along Boston's shoreline. Adams Street extends south from the area that would become the early core of Dorchester, around Meeting House Hill, down to the bridge over the Neponset River at Lower Mills.

Along the street length, multiple families owned massive farm estates—often meadows and orchards on the west side of Adams Street and grasslands along the shoreline salt marshes on the east. At either end of the street were the more built-up anchors of the two cultural and economic centers of the town of Dorchester, but the area in between was relatively quiet, while also being physically well connected to these anchors.

FIGURE 30.1
Photo of the Clap-Field House around 1890, prior to its move and brick cladding (DHS 1890a; image courtesy of the DHS).

It was in this central area that the Robinson and the Clap families settled. While the Robinsons would be more visible in the Fields Corner historic record due to their ownership of more land and the longevity of their name in the area, the Robinsons and Claps married each other and together owned much of the area.

In 1772, Samuel Clap, a housewright, purchased a lot from Edward Breck in the sparsely developed area that would become Fields Corner.[1] It is likely that Samuel himself was responsible for the building of his house soon afterward. Clap built a large late Georgian house with all of the popular design elements of the time: a shallow hipped roof angling in from all four sides; prominent chimneys along the outer walls of the house; and a symmetrical facade featuring a central door, five bays of windows along the front, and four bays down the side.

A photo of the house from the late nineteenth century shows that there was also a large barn behind the house, a fence made of pudding stone and wood, and a classically inspired porch covering that probably dates to the Greek Revival period of the mid-nineteenth century (figure 30.1). It is no surprise that the house was described as a mansion in Samuel's probate in the 1820s. Until this point, the house had remained largely outside of historic documentation, though the Claps and nearby Robinson families raised children in the area and farmed the land, and intermarried on several occasions.

Samuel Clap Jr. received the house from his father's estate in 1824 but immediately sold it.[2] The house had multiple owners—including the Reed, Oliver, Burbeck, and Glover families—before it was purchased in 1838 by Isaac Field.[3]

In 1804, Boston had laid out Dorchester Avenue, a straight highway connecting Boston directly to Lower Mills. It crossed the far older Adams Street at an oblique angle, creating a distinctly narrow intersection. Here, early industries sprang up as the crossroad brought with it new economic opportunities. It was also, coincidentally, the precise location of the Clap-Field House, which had been standing in a relatively quiet area of Dorchester but now it was just to the east of the intersection. Though this radically changed the landscape of the region, it also increased the visibility of the stately home.

Near his new home at the intersection, Isaac Field and his brother, Enos, opened a general store. The presence of the store and the entire Field family, which then had over five households in the immediate vicinity of the intersection, resulted in the area's gaining the name of Field's Corner. The intersection's name later lost the apostrophe and became Fields Corner.

In the late 1880s, the Field family moved the Clap-Field House to the rear of the lot and built a large brick commercial building on the street (figure 30.2). In the 1890s, the Field family decided to sell the entire property, and it passed into the ownership of Patrick O'Hearn. He converted the brick building, the narrow addition on the rear, and the connected Clap-Field

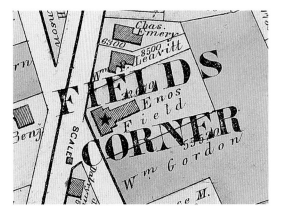

House into a massive storage facility, adding the current brick cladding to the house around 1918.[4] A recent examination by Historic Boston Incorporated revealed that the house retains many of its original interior features.[5] The Clap-Field House has no state or federal historic designations and is not a Boston Landmark.

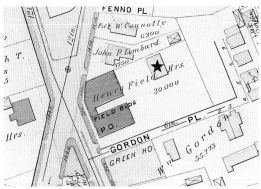

FIGURE 30.2 Maps in atlases from 1874 (top) and 1894 (bottom), showing the Clap-Field House (the red stars) before and after its move (Hopkins 1874 and G. W. Bromley and Co. 1894; images courtesy of the Norman B. Leventhal Map Center, edits by author).

# 31. Warren Tavern

2 Pleasant Street, Charlestown | Ca. 1780

John Langdon, a future signer of the Constitution, reflected via letter upon the burning of Charlestown on June 17, 1775: "The low, mean revenge and wanton cruelty of the ministerial sons of tyranny, in burning the pleasant town of Charlestown, beggars all description."[1] When the smoke cleared after the battle, Charlestown lay in ruins, having been burned by the incendiary artillery fired upon it from Copp's Hill and ships in Boston Harbor in revenge for the rebel fortifications that had appeared overnight on Breed's Hill.

After the battle, the people of Charlestown returned to their city to rebuild. In 1780, John Leach drew the "Plan of the New Streets of Charlestown with the Alterations of the Old," the first map of the town as it began to rebuild.[2] In it, he provided the first documentation of the existence of Warren Tavern, Charlestown's first postwar tavern. It was built by Eliphalet Newell, a local baker and Freemason who had served as an officer in the Massachusetts artillery in 1775–77. He may also have participated in the Boston Tea Party.[3]

Taverns, also called ordinaries, were common fixtures of a community. They were places where one could find food and beverages, most also rented rooms for travelers, and all were meeting places for community members. This became especially important during the lead-up to the Revolution. Before the war, the most famous tavern in Charlestown was the Three Cranes Tavern, which had started its life as the 1629 great house of John Winthrop. It remained standing until it was burned during the Battle of Bunker Hill. As a symbol of the tavern's significance to the community, the residents of Charlestown chose to leave the site of the Three Cranes Tavern permanently undeveloped, to host a market and be a memorial of what their town had lost during the war.

The Warren Tavern was one of the first buildings to be built in Charlestown after the fire, and it is the oldest remaining building in the neighborhood. The tavern had three stories of combined commercial (dining) and rental rooms. Its architecture is relatively unremarkable, representing a practical version of late Georgian style with a hipped roof like many other structures of the period and a symmetrical front facade on the Pleasant Street side of the building.

Like all taverns, it had a prominent sign out front representing its name both as a landmark and as a guide for illiterate residents. Historic records show that the Warren Tavern's sign depicted General Joseph Warren in full Masonic regalia.[4] Warren had been mortally wounded during the Battle of Bunker Hill, and the tavern was named in his honor. The Masonic regalia also hinted at the activities that occurred inside.

In 1784, Charlestown residents established the King Solomon's Lodge of the Masons in Warren Tavern. Members of the lodge initially met inside the main building and later in a hall built for them in 1786 behind the tavern. Paul Revere (see building #2) was a signer of the lodge's charter and a frequent guest lecturer. The lodge was also instrumental in raising the first monument to the Battle of Bunker Hill. Erected in 1794 in City Square, in the form of a wooden Tuscan pillar, it was later rebuilt in marble and placed inside the current Bunker Hill Monument structure.[5]

In addition to its Masonic and tavern use, the Warren Tavern served as an early meeting place for town selectmen, making it also a political and legal setting—a common way that early taverns functioned in colonial Boston. The tavern remained an important local institution for several decades until 1813, when it closed.[6]

In 1899, the elevated railroad entered Charlestown, creating a massive iron structure along Main Street and greatly affecting the view of the many historic homes and businesses along the street (figure 31.1). The Warren Tavern did not become rental housing, as many of the buildings in this book did toward the end of the nineteenth century. Instead, it was used for other commercial purposes including as a private club, a bakery, and a storage warehouse.

The tavern remained a warehouse into the twentieth century. By the 1960s, it had been abandoned and boarded up. In 1971 James River Adams began a full restoration of the Warren Tavern as part of a years-long restoration project involving five nearby historic properties in what was known as the Thompson Triangle (including buildings #43–44 and 46–47). In 1972 Alan and Ann Cunha and Neil and Ed Grenan purchased the property and reopened the Warren Tavern to the public.[7] Though the building is on the National Register, it is not a designated Boston Landmark. The Warren Tavern remains a popular food and drink destination for both locals and tourists in Charlestown.

FIGURE 31.1
View of the Warren Tavern in 1970, before renovations and the removal of the elevated railroad on Main Street in Charlestown (BLC 1970b; image courtesy of the City of Boston Archives).

In 1782, near the end of the Revolution, Major John Jones Spooner paid for the construction of a large Georgian-style house with a broad symmetrical front facade, multiple chimneys, and a shallow hipped roof. Spooner's wealth is suggested by the balustrade railing around the peak of the roof and the small man-made elevated platform that the house sits on.

Spooner sold the house to Captain William Lambert in 1788. During the Revolution, Lambert had conducted business in Halifax, Nova Scotia, where he acted as an agent for American prisoners taken there after being captured during battle. From 1775 to 1778, he was responsible for supplying provisions for these imprisoned Americans. However, when the British felt that Lambert was being too sympathetic to the imprisoned rebels, he was forced to quickly flee Canada, and he returned to Boston in 1788.[1]

In the same year, Lambert chose Roxbury as his place of retirement and bought the Spooner estate (figure 32.1). Spooner appears to have let his property remain relatively natural, and Lambert refers to his new thirteen-acre property in a letter as a wilderness. During his family's thirty-five-year occupancy of the house, he is credited with major landscape changes, including the removal of stone walls, bedrock outcrops (via blasting), and dense vegetation.[2] Lambert's additions to the house include the large Federal-style large front porch, with its classically inspired columns, and a large landscaped yard.

The house passed on to the Taber family in the nineteenth century, but the evolution of Roxbury from a rural suburb of Boston to a bustling industrial hub during the nineteenth century put pressure on the large estates to divide into rental properties. The house's position close to the street probably saved

FIGURE 32.1 A 1799 painting of the First Church in Roxbury and surrounding area, showing the Spooner-Lambert House (the yellow house on the far left) and the Dillaway-Thomas House (the yellow house on the far right; see building #22) (Penniman 1799; image courtesy of the Art Institute of Chicago).

it from being seen as in the way of development, which encroached upon it on all sides.

In the twentieth century, the house became home to various institutions, including the Roxbury Home for Aged Women from 1904 to 1951.[3] By the end of the twentieth century, a bank had foreclosed on the house, and its future was uncertain. In the summer of 1992, Historic Boston Incorporated (HBI) purchased the property and set about sensitively restoring the exterior of the house, as well as its significant remaining interior architectural elements, and adaptively reusing the house by converting the former single-family mansion into four separate apartments.[4] The rental proceeds supported the important work of HBI until the organization chose to convert the building into condominiums in 2000, selling all four apartments to the people who were already renting them.[5] Though the house is not a Boston Landmark, it is on the National Register. HBI placed a preservation easement on the house's deed, which will fundamentally prevent insensitive modifications of the house and surviving landscape by future owners.

# 33. Bicknell House

51 Minot Street, Dorchester | Ca. 1785

The Bicknell House is one of several in this book (including the one discussed in building #42) whose move from its original location has shrouded much of its history. Moving a house was not particularly uncommon in the eighteenth and nineteenth centuries. For example, the 1895 move of the Blake House (building #1) never made the papers. In 1894 alone, Boston's City Council approved contractors' requests to move fifty-two buildings in the city.[1] Though the records state the street where the houses stood, they do not name the owners of the buildings or state where the buildings were moved to.

In the southern end of Dorchester—near the mouth of the Neponset River and east of Lower Mills Village—the Adams and Neponset villages were formed. The villages were located at major Dorchester crossroads, including Neponset and Adams Streets and the roads going from the two bridges over the Neponset River and going to Milton and Quincy. Minot Street, laid out in 1805, served as the direct overland route between the two villages.[2]

In 1810, John Bicknell purchased an undeveloped lot on Minot Street from the Pierce family, whose large historic estate (see building #3) is located just to the northwest of this property.[3] It appears that instead of building a new house, Bicknell chose to move an older house to his property sometime after 1810. According to one source, the *Dorchester Book*, John Bicknell's house originally "stood on the upper road [Washington Street] and is only part of the original structure."[4]

Unfortunately, Washington Street is one of the longest in Dorchester, with numerous eighteenth-century homes that could have been the origin of the

Bicknell House. There is not enough information currently available to determine which house on Washington was the origin of this house fragment.

Stylistically, the Bicknell House has a subdued Georgian gambrel roof with a five-bay front facade and three second-story dormers, all of which are typical of modest homes from around the time of the Revolution (figure 33.1).

Since most ells are typically younger than the main houses to which they are attached (see building #40 for an exception), it is likely that this house may have once belonged to an even earlier seventeenth- or eighteenth-century building on Washington Street, but that still leaves many buildings as its possible origin.

Somewhat ironically, the Bicknell House, itself an addition or ell, had two ells attached to it in the nineteenth century. It retains the western ell today. It is likely that the position of the house at the very front of its lot, the relatively small size of the lot, and the overall small scale of many of the houses on Minot Street has resulted in this house's avoiding the development pressures seen elsewhere in Dorchester so far. The house has no historic designations.

In 1786, just three years after Massachusetts abolished slavery, two Black men purchased an undeveloped lot of land on the corner of Pinckney and Joy Streets on Beacon Hill. In the late eighteenth century, many free Black Bostonians chose to move to the north slope of Beacon Hill, often moving from a historically Black village on the north slope of Copp's Hill in the North End and creating a new and now historically Black neighborhood. Despite its close proximity to the core of downtown Boston, the steep slope of Boston's tri-mountain hills (or Tremont), just north of Boston Common, resulted in a relatively long delay in the development of what would become the Beacon Hill neighborhood.

Colonel George Middleton and Louis Glapion built the house at 5 Pinckney Street between 1786 and 1787. Middleton was a free Black man who had played an important role during the Revolution as the leader of the Bucks of America, an all-Black rebel militia company. Though much of the function of the militia was poorly recorded, it is believed that their functions included the guarding of Boston merchants' property in the city during the Revolution—possibly including the property of enslavers.[1]

Professionally, Middleton was a horse tender—someone who was hired to care for some of the many horses necessary for transportation in Boston at the time.[2] Middleton was also an abolitionist and early member of the Prince Hall

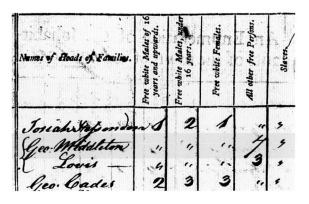

FIGURE 34.2 Detail of the 1790 US census entry for the Middleton-Glapion family, showing both men and their wives counted together as one family with George Middleton listed as head of household (United States Census Bureau 1790; edits by author).

Masons, a historically Black Masonic lodge, and he became grand master of the African Masonic Lodge.[3] In 1796, he helped organize the Boston African Benevolent Society, whose mission was to support Black communities facing white resistance to integration.[4] Middleton also fought for equal rights to education for Black children in Boston beginning in 1800, though the first Black school in the city (the Abiel Smith School, on Joy Street) did not open until 1835. Glapion's history is less well recorded, but he is known to have been a hairdresser who was probably born in the French West Indies.

The two men added two other buildings (at 1 and 3 Pinckney Street) to their home, extending the structures across their property east to the corner of Joy Street, the core of the free Black community in Boston. The two later buildings functioned as additions to the main house at 5 Pinckney Street.[5]

The oldest building in Beacon Hill, that main house is a modest wooden structure with four-bays and two stories—one of just eleven wooden buildings in the predominantly brick neighborhood (figure 34.1). Currently, the house has double front doors, but it is likely that only the eastern (right) door is original. There is a large late-nineteenth-century dormer on the third floor roofline, which gives the property a three-story appearance. This two-story wooden building would have been similar to many of the homes built by Black Bostonians on the north slope of Beacon Hill in the late eighteenth and early nineteenth centuries.

Middleton and his wife, Elsey Marsh, moved into the house with Glampion. In 1793, Glapion married Lucy Hawkins, and all four lived in the house together. Neither couple had children.[6] In the 1790 census, the four Black men and women in the home are recorded as a single-family household, with Middleton listed as the head of household (figure 34.2). A nineteenth-century account by Lydia Child, their former neighbor on Pinckney Street, states that "his morals were questioned,—he was passionate, intemperate, and profane."[7] The living arrangement of Middleton and Glapion, coupled with historic re-

FIGURE 34.3
A 1934 image from
the Pinckney Club's
Christmas card
(HNE 1934; image
courtesy of HNE).

cords and accounts, have led to the theory that the two men were a gay couple.[8]

Glapion died in 1813, leaving his share of the 1, 3, and 5 Pinckney Street property to Lucy. Middleton survived his wife, Elsey, dying in 1815 and leaving his half of the property to his "good friend Tristan Babcock."[9] It appears that 5 Pinckney Street went to Babcock, as he sold this property in 1817 to David Shillaber, who operated a dry goods store in downtown Boston. Lucy eventually also sold her share (1 and 3 Pinckney Street) to Shillaber, whose family retained ownership of the three buildings into the 1920s—apparently renting it to others, as the Shillaber family's primary home appears to have been first in the South End and later in Brighton.[10]

In 1855, the three properties were transformed with the demolition of 3 Pinckney, the middle structure, and its replacement with a four-story brick building more similar in character to the surrounding row houses. In the 1930s, 5 Pinckney Street became the Pinckney Club, a private establishment, and 1 Pinckney Street became an Italian restaurant that catered to Boston's bohemian residents (figure 34.3). Today, 5 Pinckney Street is a private home that is a Boston Landmark as a contributing building in the Historic Beacon Hill Architectural District, a National Historic Landmark, and a stop on Boston's Black Heritage Trail.

# 35. Fowler-Clark-Epstein Farm

487 Norfolk Street, Mattapan | Ca. 1786

The Fowler-Clark-Epstein Farm is a rare example of a post-Revolution farmhouse within a Massachusetts city. According to a recent survey, it is one of only twelve remaining farmhouses from this period in urban contexts, and of those, it may be the earliest.[1]

In 1786, Samuel Fowler inherited a portion of his grandfather's 330-acre colonial land grant. Samuel's estate consisted of thirty-five acres and a barn on Norfolk Street, an early Dorchester road that connected the northern portions of Washington Street in Dorchester to the Mattapan area mills. At the time of Fowler's inheritance, this area was an undeveloped rural space almost equidistant from the more urban cores of Mattapan Village (Dorchester), Lower Mills Village (Dorchester), and Roxbury. It was here, in Dorchester's rural landscape, that Fowler and his wife, Mary, built a farmhouse and raised their family.

The farmhouse has five bays, a central entrance, and central fireplace. Its roof is a shallow gable, unlike many of the post-Revolution gambrels popular in the surrounding area. At two stories, with an attic, it is quite a bit larger than several other houses in this portion of the book, but that is likely due to the overall size of Fowler's family, the fact that the farm setting allowed for larger structures, and Fowler's relative wealth as a farmer with considerable land holdings.

Fowler died in 1810, leaving his wife a smaller eleven-acre parcel including the Fowler-Clark-Epstein house and barn. Mary sold the property to her son, Samuel Fowler Jr. After he died, the property was divided into seven parts and left to various family members. Beginning in 1822, Samuel Baker, another farmer, and his wife, Patience, began purchasing these parts from the Fowler family, eventually accumulating six-sevenths of the eleven acres via auction. They did not keep the property for long, however, selling the house and farm in 1824 to Daniel Sanderson, another Dorchester farmer. He was eventually able to purchase the last seventh of the land from Fowler's descendants.[2]

In 1837, Sanderson sold the Fowler farm to Mary and Henry Clark, whose family and descendants owned the property until 1940. Though the arrival of street cars in the nineteenth century brought increased development at various intersections and commercial cores, when the Clark family purchased the property in the 1830s, much of Norfolk Street's central expanse still supported large rural farms.

Two major changes occurred to the property during the nineteenth century. First was the addition to the northwest of the property in the 1860s of a new building in ornate Victorian style that served as a stable and carriage house and that remains today. Second was the addition of Hosmer Street on the

northern end of the property. Multiple subdivisions of the property in the 1900s reduced the property to just under an acre.[3]

In 1941, Jorge and Ida Epstein bought the property, and their family remained its owners and occupants throughout the remainder of the twentieth century. Changes to the property made by the Epsteins in the mid-twentieth century include the addition of wooden shingles on the farmhouse on top of the original clapboard siding and a large hall-like addition to the rear of the original farmhouse (figure 35.1).[4]

On April 12, 2005, the Epstein family requested a permit from the City of Boston to demolish the farmhouse and build twenty-two town houses on the property. The request was reviewed by the BLC through its Article 85 process (see the introduction), which voted to invoke the ninety-day demolition delay, temporarily halting the demolition. During this period, neighbors and other Dorchester residents submitted a petition to the BLC to designate the farm a Boston Landmark. Three days before the demolition delay expired, the BLC voted in favor of a ninety-day temporary Landmark designation, which allowed for the completion of a Study Report. On September 6, 2005, the BLC awarded the property full Landmark status.

In 2015, Historic Boston Incorporated purchased the property from the Epstein family and began a restoration of the property, which was finished in 2018. In 2020, the buildings were added to the National Register. Today, the property is home to the Urban Farming Institute, an organization devoted to training urban farmers and developing additional farms throughout Boston. The Fowler-Clark-Epstein Farm buildings provide a classroom and meeting spaces, as well as a demonstration kitchen, farm stand, and greenhouse for residents of the Mattapan neighborhood of Boston to learn about and enjoy the produce grown in the new farming beds created at the front and rear of the historic farmhouse.

# 36. Elijah Jones House

3 Marcy Road, Mattapan  |  Ca. 1786

FIGURE 36.1 The Elijah Jones House prior to its move (the red star in the upper left), the Neponset River, and downtown Mattapan village in 1890. The Tileston and Hollingsworth Paper Mill is labeled 10 (in the lower center) (O. H. Bailey and Co. 1890a; image courtesy of the Norman B. Leventhal Map Center, edits by author).

In March 1777, the housewright Elijah Jones purchased one and three-quarter acres of undeveloped pasture from the town of Dorchester. The property was on the north side of what would become River Street in Mattapan, near the heart of the millworks along the nearby Neponset River (figure 36.1).[1] When Jones sold the property in 1786, it was divided into two parcels—one containing a house and other buildings and the other containing the blacksmith shop of Jones's brother, Thomas.[2] It is likely that Elijah built both structures during the Revolution.

Elijah Jones's house is modest in scale, with a gambrel roof and a single story. It has a central doorway with three (probably not original) window openings in its gambrel roof, and it currently has a central chimney that has almost certainly been greatly reduced in size. The mills immediately to the south of this house on the Neponset River included the paper-making factory of Hugh McLean, an Irish immigrant, and James Boise. McLean purchased both lots from Jones in 1786 and left his estate to his wife, Agnes, and their son, John, in 1800.[3]

John McLean was a wealthy Boston merchant. Upon his death in 1823, he left his wife, Ann, their house and $35,000 and gave Harvard University money to fund a named chair, the McLean Professor of Ancient and Modern History. The chair is currently occupied by Emma Dench, a Roman historian and Dame Judi Dench's niece. McLean's will also included funds for the Massachusetts General Hospital (MGH). The world-renowned McLean Hospital, a psychiatric facility in Belmont, Massachusetts, is named in his honor.[4]

McLean left $50,000 to Jonathan and Francis Amory—Ann's brother and cousin, respectively—as trustees, to invest and provide the proceeds to Ann. Upon her death, the remaining funds were to be divided between Harvard and MGH. In 1828, the funds were distributed to those institutions, which sued the trustees in 1830—claiming that the investments had been diminished due to speculation and negligence. The Massachusetts Supreme Judicial Court found the trustees not liable for the losses, but the court clarified that although investments can lead to losses, money in trust should not be invested speculatively. This became known as the prudent man rule, which holds that when a trust is not left money in terms that specify which types of investments are permitted, the trust must act as a prudent man would in investing his own property.[5]

John McLean's will gave the Jones house and shop to John Boies, the son of James Boies, Hugh McLean's business partner. Because John Boies died before John McLean, the house instead went to MGH. The hospital had no use for it and sold it in 1824 to Amasa Fuller, another papermaker.[6]

Fuller died in 1826. His will placed the property in trust with Thomas Crehore, an early manufacturer of playing cards, and Henry Gardner, who were to sell it within three years and split the profits with Fuller's wife.[7] Crehore was a well-known manufacturer with a factory on River Street in Mattapan. Gardner married into the Clap family and became the treasurer for Massachusetts.

Crehore and Gardner sold the house in 1827 to Isaac and Caroline Bowen, who raised their daughter, Caroline, there.[8] In 1845, the younger Caroline married Woodman Jones, a cabinetmaker trained in Dorchester by George Haynes (see building #37), who probably used the shop for his cabinetmaking business.[9] Caroline inherited the house and sold it in 1847 to Edmund Tileston, the nephew of Charles Tileston (see building #28), and Mark Hollingsworth, who together owned the Tileston and Hollingsworth Paper Mill (figure 36.1).[10] The deed states that the property still contained a house and a cabinet shop with outbuildings.

Tileston and Hollingsworth had purchased the McCarney and Leeds paper mill in Mattapan in 1831 and were major property owners in the area. They probably rented out the house and shop until they sold both to Joseph Whitney, a millwright.[11] The house was still in the Whitney family when it was moved in 1907 to the new Marcy Road (then named Whitney Park).[12] The house's original site was then occupied by a three-story multifamily home, which has since been demolished. The site is now an undeveloped parcel owned by the city.

It is probable that the move saved the house, placing it on a dead-end side street with modest single-family houses of similar size—an area that has not yet experienced pressure for redevelopment. The house is not a Boston Landmark or on the National Register, but fortunately there are few threats to its preservation at the moment.

In 1788, Massachusetts became the sixth state to join the United States of America, and Samuel Crehore built his home in Dorchester on a quarter-acre vacant lot purchased from Ezra Badlam (see building #28), his father-in-law.

Crehore's house is a house in the transitional Georgian-Federal style. Prior to the mid-nineteenth-century addition of its massive Greek Revival-style triangular gable, it probably had a hipped roof similar to those of neighboring buildings of slightly later date (figure 37.1).

After Samuel Crehore's death, the property passed to John Shepherd Crehore in 1805.[1] At the time, it included the house, a barn, and a shop. John Crehore was a chair maker, and his son Lemuel and grandson Charles became national leaders in the paper industries that grew up along the Neponset River between Lower Mills and Mattapan (figure 37.2). Charles was also a celebrated medic who served Union troops during the Civil War.[2]

FIGURE 37.1
Digital recreation of a hipped roof on the George Haynes House (photo and edits by author).

The house's ownership by John Crehore was brief, and by the end of the year, the house was in the possession of John Hawes.[3] Hawes was a wealthy farmer who is said to have "had a limited acquaintance with men and manners."[4] He married into the Clapp family and then retired with his wife to South Boston, where his 1805 brick mansion still stands as the oldest house in South Boston.[5]

Hawes retained ownership of the house in Dorchester until 1815, when he sold it to Captain Henry Cox and Edmund Baker.[6] Both men were involved in the manufacturing of paper in the many paper mills along the Neponset at the time. Cox bought out Baker's ownership in 1816 and either lived in the house or rented it out.[7] In 1824, Cox sold the property to Walter Baker of the Walter Baker Chocolate Factory.[8]

In 1818, Baker became a partner in the mill businesses of his father, Edmund Baker.[9] In the same year that Walter purchased the Haynes House, Edmund retired and left the businesses to Walter. Walter became a major figure in the town of Dorchester around this time, and as a successful businessman, he expanded his father's mill industry from its beginning in a single modest mill building to a complex of buildings covering over forty acres of land that was on both sides of the Neponset.[10] In 1836, Walter Baker sold the Haynes House to George Haynes, and it is George's name that appears on earliest maps—resulting in his association with the house in historic building in-

FIGURE 37.2
Aerial image show-
ing the location of
the George Haynes
House (the red star)
in Lower Mills (O.
H. Bailey and Co.
1890b; image cour-
tesy of the Norman
B. Leventhal Map
Center, edits by
author).

ventories.[11] Haynes owned multiple properties along Washington Street in the mid-nineteenth century. His wealth came from his nearby store, George Haynes and Sons Stove Store, which was located just north of his home on Washington Street. Most recently, the Haynes House was the home of the Milton Funeral Home (now closed), and the house has multiple twentieth-century additions. Today, the property and two others adjacent to it are owned by developers.

In 2014, planning began to develop 1126 Washington Street and the surrounding properties into a large condominium complex. The plans include the demolition of the George Haynes House and two neighboring properties, none of which are currently Landmark designated or have other historic designations or protections. As of the writing of this book, the plans remain in progress.

# 38. Brighton First Church Parsonage

4–10 Academy Hill Road, Brighton  |  Ca. 1790

For its parsonage, Brighton's First Church purchased a lot on Academy Hill Road that was to the south of the church and a short walk away. The exact style of the original structure is difficult to determine due to recent additions, but it probably had a central chimney and entrance flanked by window bays in a late Georgian or early Federal style.

Soon after it was built, the parsonage became the home of the Reverend John Foster and his wife, Hannah Webster Foster, who moved there from the Ebenezer Smith House (see building #10).[1] It was here that in 1797 Hannah wrote *The Coquette; or, The History of Eliza Wharton* (figure 38.1), becoming the first American-born woman to publish a book.[2] Hannah Foster chose to publish anonymously as "a lady of Massachusetts," due to the controversial nature of her story.

The plot of the book is laid out a series of letters that tell a fictionalized version of the story of Elizabeth Whitman, the daughter of a prominent pastor in Hartford, Connecticut. She became pregnant out of wedlock, gave birth to a stillborn child in a tavern, and then died.

The scandalous story was the second-most popular book (after the Bible) in New England in the early nineteenth century and "one of the two best-selling American novels" of the previous century.[3] The story follows Eliza Wharton, who is caught in a desperate love triangle between two men: an uninteresting but safe clergyman and a confirmed bachelor who refuses to let anyone else have Eliza. Eliza loses both men to her indecision, and by the time she changes her mind, both men have already married. Eliza has an affair with the formerly confirmed bachelor that results in an illegitimate pregnancy. Overcome by guilt over the affair and pregnancy, Eliza flees, eventually dying while giving birth to a stillborn child.

Though one of the most significant figures in American publishing history, Hannah Foster was not credited in print as the author of the book until 1866, twenty-six years after her death. Foster wrote a second book, *The Boarding School; or, Lessons of a Preceptress to Her Pupils* (also known as *The Boarding House*), in 1798 while living in the house on Academy Hill Road, though it did not attract nearly as much attention as her first novel. After publishing her books, Foster continued writing for the local newspaper and taught

FIGURE 38.1
The cover of the 1855 edition of *The Coquette* (Foster 1855; image courtesy of University of California Libraries via archives.org).

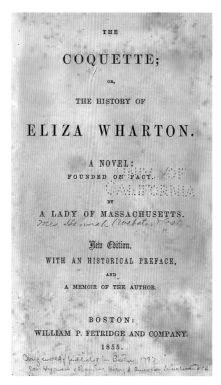

FIGURE 38.2
View of the
parsonage from
the south, showing
portions of the
original eighteenth-
century roofline
with the later
entablature added
across the gable,
creating a Greek
Revival–style
pediment (photo
by author).

writing while raising her family. She remained active in the community and is credited with founding the first women's club in Massachusetts, in the early 1800s. After her husband's death, Foster went to live with her daughter in Montreal, where she died in 1840.[4]

The Brighton parsonage underwent extreme modifications in the nineteenth and twentieth centuries. The house stopped being used as a parsonage around 1840. It was soon updated in the Greek Revival style, resulting in the creation of the prominent pediment on the gable end of the house (figure 38.2). There were large additions to the rear and front of the building. These included the large storefronts on the front of the house that completely cover the original front facade. Today, these are two-story brick commercial spaces.

The only visible portion of the original structure can be seen from a nearby parking lot. Even here, the end of the house has had a new entrance added to the facade, as well as the Greek Revival pediment. This property remains a nationally significant historic property that could be restored to much of its original eighteenth-century appearance. The Brighton First Church Parsonage is part of a National Register historic district but is not a Boston Landmark.

# 39. Bond-Glover House

35 Humphreys Street, Dorchester  |  Ca. 1790

The Bond-Glover House appears to have been built soon after 1787, when John Holbrook of Killingly, Connecticut, sold eleven acres of pasture along a road that would eventually be named Humphreys Street.[1] The buyer, Ebenezer Kilton Jr., and his wife, Abigail Bird, were a farming family who funded the construction of a modest two-story building with a gambrel roof and front face three bays wide by one bay deep. The couple were married in 1789 and were survived by four children.[2]

Kilton sold the land to Jacob Beal in 1799,[3] at which point the property was just a half-acre in size and contained houses and outbuildings, including a communal barn shared by neighboring properties. It appears that both the Bond-Glover House and the Kilton-Beal House (see building #40) were part of this half-acre parcel and that both houses were built sometime around 1790.

After Beal died in 1810, the court sold his estate to pay his debts and funeral expenses. The house was sold in two halves in 1810 and 1813, with Asa Richardson as the buyer both times.[4] He used the house as an investment property before selling it in 1827 to William Cranch Bond (figure 39.1).[5]

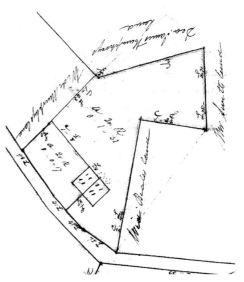

FIGURE 39.1
An image of a deed
from 1827, showing
the divided Bond-
Glover House
on its original lot
(Norfolk County,
*Norfolk Registry of
Deeds* 82:271 and 272;
image courtesy of
familysearch.org).

Bond owned the house from 1827 to 1837 and also used it as an investment property. He lived with his wife, Selinda, and their six children in a large home nearby on Cottage Street.

Bond's father, William Bond, founded an important clock-making business that became William Bond and Son when William Cranch Bond joined it. This company remained in business until 1977 and is credited with creating the first American-made chronometers—clocks that worked on boats.

William Cranch Bond was also an amateur astronomer who independently discovered the Great Comet of 1811—before word reached the United States that a French astronomer had first found the comet. He amassed a large collection of astronomical observation instruments, and the parlor of his Dorchester house was reported to have a retractable ceiling for his massive home telescope.[6]

In 1839, he was commissioned by the US Navy to measure longitude and collect other scientific data in support of the nation's efforts to explore the Pacific Ocean. In the same year, Harvard University, recognizing the value of his talents and observation equipment, appointed him its official astronomical observer and relocated his personal observatory to the university. Bond and his son George made multiple astronomical discoveries there.[7]

The public fascination with Bond's observatory allowed Harvard to amass the funds to build a larger telescope, which resulted in the two men's first observations of Saturn's eighth moon and its inner rings.[8] William Cranch Bond's later important inventions included a clock synchronizer, which aided in the prevention of train wrecks.[9] William Bond and Son's clocks and chronometers can be found in historic scientific collections around the world, including at the Smithsonian Institution. Harvard's Collection of Historical Scientific Instruments includes a group of William Cranch Bond's clocks, chronometers, and observation equipment, as well as an archive containing Bond's personal records and photographs—including deeds and other information that may be related to the Bond-Glover House. A crater on the moon is named in Bond's honor.[10]

James Glover bought the house from Bond in 1837, and it remained in the Glover family until around 1910, when the southwestern portion of the property was sold off and developed.[11] The Bond-Glover House has undergone considerable modifications over the years, and vinyl siding now hides any remaining eighteenth-century elements of the house other than its overall shape. It is not listed on the National Register, nor is it a Boston Landmark.

# 40. Kilton-Beal House

29 Humphreys Street, Dorchester  |  Ca. 1790

Until the mid-nineteenth century, the Kilton-Beal House shared the history of the Bond-Glover House (see building #39). Like its neighbor, the Kilton-Beal House had a gabled roof with a central chimney, a five-bay front facade, and a relatively thin one-bay depth. But unlike its neighbor, it was oriented at an angle to the road.

When the Kilton-Beal House was sold in 1799 to Jacob Beal, it was the eastern house on the half-acre parcel that included the Bond-Glover House. It would remain in the Beal family until the early twentieth century.[1]

Sometime during the mid-nineteenth century, the Beal family added a large Greek Revival house to the front of the property, turning the older structure into ell (figure 40.1).

In the early 2000s, the western portion of the property, having remained undeveloped for centuries, was chosen as the site of a long three-story multi-family home. This property has not been listed on the National Register, nor is it a Boston Landmark. Its significance lies in its history as an early agricultural building in close proximity to Boston's urban core; its close proximity to another eighteenth-century house with which it shares a history; and its later additions, which represent the transitions in Dorchester's architectural styles in the eighteenth, nineteenth, and twenty-first centuries.

FIGURE 41.1 Map in an 1918 atlas showing the Calvin Bird House (outlined in red), encroaching development, and additions on the Dudley Street side of property that abuts the front of the house (G. W. Bromley and Co. 1918; image courtesy of the Norman B. Leventhal Map Center, edits by author).

Tracing the history of this house is difficult due to its connection to the Bird family, whose members owned multiple parcels in the surrounding area. The house was probably built sometime around 1790, based on its shallow hipped roof and large central chimney, but little of its exterior remains, and the house appears to have avoided early photography. Nor does it seem to appear in deeds until 1824, when Nancy Bird purchased two and a quarter acres of land from Lemuel Foster, including the house and barn. It is not clear where Foster got the house.[1]

The Bird family had been in Dorchester since Thomas Bird arrived on the second voyage of the *Mary and John* in 1635. Their large seventeenth-century home with eighteenth-century additions stood at 41 Humphreys Street, immediately to the west to the Bond-Glover House (see building #39) for much of their existence. In the 1930s, the Bird house was demolished, and a smaller single-family home and multiple three-deckers now stand in its place.

It is possible that Nancy Bird and her husband, Joseph, raised their son, Charles, in the Calvin Bird House, but it was Calvin Bird who next purchased the front half of the property from Nancy with the house on it in 1854 and the rear half of the property in 1857. The two Bird family branches are likely related, but their exact relationship between is unclear. Calvin married Mary Homer in 1848, which suggests that the property may have been purchased for the couple and their future family.[2] As the owner of the house when the first maps were drawn with owners' names listed, Calvin Bird's name became associated with this building on official historic building forms. Mary took over the property after Calvin died in 1895.[3]

Facing pressure from developers and the rapid increase in Dorchester's population at the end of the nineteenth century, Mary Bird began to divide the rear of the property into smaller building lots along Wendover Street. Before and after Mary's death in 1910, she and her heirs added wooden storefronts to the Dudley Street side of the property that obscured the house, as shown in maps from 1904 and 1918.[4] It is probable that Mary's heirs saw the value of the property in terms not of a personal home, but of real estate located on a major route between Dorchester and Roxbury. Despite their impact on the front of the house, the addition of buildings there—which likely included significant modifications to the home's original front facade—would have been financially beneficial.

Subsequent atlases and aerial images reveal the encroachment of the buildings on the Dudley Street facade, up to and including the entirety of the Bird House (figure 41.1). The Calvin Bird House was demolished in the summer of 2021. The building had no historic designation, and all that was visible of the house to the public was a small portion of the corner of the building, its shallow hipped roof, and its large central chimney.

The Caroline Capen House is a two-story wooden house with a symmetrical five-bay Georgian facade, central chimney, and shallow hipped roof. Based on its architectural style, it was built around 1790.

Throughout the seventeenth and eighteenth centuries, the area that would become Whitfield Street was located in the rear of multiple large farming estates. Many of these were owned by the Capen family, whose early-seventeenth-century home was located on Washington Street to the east (see the Honorable Mentions). Samuel Capen was a wealthy landowner who had many acres in the central part of Dorchester. When he died in 1877, he left his entire estate to his widow, Caroline.[1]

In 1879, Caroline married Gustavus Jackson, and since she outlived him, she inherited his estate as well.[2] Although an 1884 map does not show any structure in the location of the current building, an 1889 atlas shows the house owned by Caroline Jackson on the newly planned Whitfield Street several years before Caroline died.[3] In her 1891 will, Caroline distributed her various diamonds to her relatives and turned over the rest of her estate to a trust.[4]

It is not clear where Caroline's house came from. The 1884 map shows a small house lot on Washington Street tucked into the Capen properties opposite, where Lyndhurst Street is located today (figure 42.1). Since no owner's name is given for this property, it could also have been owned by the Capens, including Caroline, in the eighteenth and nineteenth centuries. In the 1889 map, a building with an identical footprint appears on Whitfield Street, and the 1884 building has disappeared—suggesting that Washington Street is the original location of the moved house.

After Caroline's death, the property was selected as the site of the Dorchester Stables, which are built directly south of the historic house. By 1918, the house was on a separate property from the stables and had become a family home, which it remains today.[5] The house is not a designated Landmark, nor is it listed on the National Register. If it can be determined how Caroline came into possession of the house and why she chose to move it to its current location, its significance and early history may become clearer. The building may be even older than the estimated age provided here.

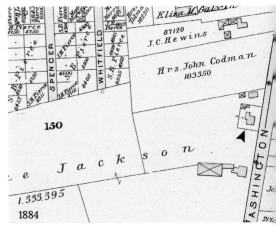

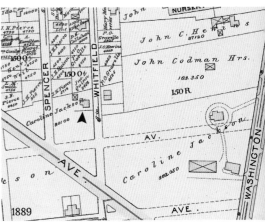

FIGURE 42.1
Maps from 1884 (top) and 1889 (bottom) atlases, showing possible original locations of the Capen House (red arrows) before its move and its location after (G. W. Bromley and Co. 1884 and 1889; image courtesy of the Norman B. Leventhal Map Center, edits by author).

# 43. Deacon John Larkin House

55–61 Main Street, Charlestown | Ca. 1790

John Larkin was both a deacon of the First Congregational Church in Boston and a tea merchant who amassed a large fortune.[1] He lost his original home down the road in the fires resulting from the Battle of Bunker Hill. Before the fires, Larkin had met Paul Revere (see building #2) in his boat at the shoreline of Charlestown and loaned him a horse—belonging to Larkin's father—to continue his midnight ride.

In 1783, Larkin purchased a small lot on Main Street from Nathan Adams and hired builders to construct a large Georgian house on the corner of what would later be Main and Winthrop Streets.[2] The house was five bays wide by five bays deep and had a symmetrical facade and central door on Main Street. Like other buildings of the period, it had a shallow hipped roof and chimneys around the outside of the building instead of a central chimney. Unlike many of its neighbors, though, it had a shallow third story, possibly to provide living space for servants.

John and his wife, Ruth, already had multiple adult children when they moved to the new house, and it appears that at least their three youngest daughters would have been raised there. Larkin left his house and land to Ruth when he died in 1808.[3] At that point, the deeds and wills fall silent for several decades about the ownership of the Larkin House.

Later deeds and historical atlases reveal that Susan Roberts, a widow, and other members of the Roberts family sold the house to the Klous family in an 1870 deed, and the Klouses retained ownership of it until around 1912.[4] This deed refers to an 1870 property plan drawing by Edward Ames that is said to be included in the deed book but does not appear there. It also refers to an earlier plan of the property drawn by Samuel M. Felton in 1831, which it says is included in the back pages of Middlesex deed book 398— but which is not there. Both of these plans would probably reveal much of the currently missing data about the owners and layout of the Larkin House between 1800 and 1860.

The Klous family made multiple small additions to the building and purchased additional adjacent buildings. Though the Klouses retained ownership of the property into the early twentieth century, the family lived out of state, which suggests that the Larkin House and adjacent buildings were now used for commercial and rental purposes and not owner occupied. By the 1970s, the building included a storefront and had asphalt siding, but it still retained many of its eighteenth-century features (figure 43.1). Though it fell into disrepair, renovations by James Rivers Adams in the early 1980s brought the building back to its former glory. It is listed on the National Register but is not a Boston Landmark. It is likely significant both because it was one of the first buildings in Boston to be built after the fires of the Battle of Bunker Hill, and because of its association with John Larkin, who assisted in an event of national significance.

# 44. John Hurd House

65–71 Main Street, Charlestown | Ca. 1790

FIGURE 44.1
The John Hurd
House as it may
have appeared
around 1790 (left)
when it was built
and around 1833
(right) when John
Hurd purchased
it and added the
third story, if it re-
mained otherwise
unchanged to the
present (photo and
edits by author).

Deacon John Larkin's 1780s land-buying spree in Charlestown resulted in his ownership of the north side of Main Street from what is today Winthrop Street to Monument Street.[1] Larkin appears to have had his own home at the corner of Winthrop and Main Streets (see building #43), and he may have also funded the construction of what would become the John Hurd House at the opposite end of his property on Main Street. As in the case of the Larkin House, the exact construction date of the Hurd House is not clear.

Sometime around 1790, builders constructed a large, nearly square two-story house with five bays on each side and with the main entrance and wider side of the house facing Main Street. The house they built is late Georgian in style, with broad windows and doorways, symmetrical facades, and a rare flat deck-on-hip roof. The corner block-like quoins are probably part of the original decorative exterior elements of the building (figure 44.1).

John Hurd purchased the building for his family home in 1833, several decades after it was first built. Hurd was a wealthy merchant who traded in West Indies goods and had an office in the relatively new 1825 Quincy Market downtown. In the early nineteenth century, probably around 1833 when he bought the house, Hurd funded the raising of its roof to allow for the addition of the third story (figure 44.1). The corner quoins increase slightly in size from the second to third story, marking this addition.[2]

The Hurd House reached a literal turning point in 1868, when the construction of Monument Street required the house to be moved. The Hurd family chose instead to rotate the house 90 degrees clockwise and move it eight feet closer to the Larkin House to make room for the street.[3] At the same time, the Hurd family moved out but retained ownership of the house, converting it into commercial space and apartments.[4]

To accommodate the rotation and new function of the house, the Hurds filled in the original front entrance and two flanking windows, all of which were now facing Monument Street. The first-floor living space was converted into multiple commercial spaces, and there was a small addition at the rear of the property. The parlors and kitchen spaces were gutted, a process that included removing most of the interior walls and replacing structural components with iron supports. The upper floors were split into two apartments, and the floors of the first story were lowered sixteen inches to make more room in the first-floor commercial space. In recent renovations, evidence of this lowering was found—including open mortises and sawed-off tenons along the frame of the house from the lowered floor.[5]

John Rand moved into the building, selling furs, hats, trunks, and furnishings out of 71 Main Street (the storefront closest to the street corner) while living above the shop. He occupied this space from around the time of the 1868 conversion of the property to 1885. Around 1870, William Murray and Son opened a dry goods store in 67 and 69 Main Street. Like Rand, the Murrays remained in the property for many years, and they eventually bought the Hurd House in 1879 from John Hurd's children. In 1922 or 1923, Donovan and Fallon Pharmacists purchased the house from the Murrays. By then, there were three separate apartments above the two first-floor commercial spaces.[6]

Around 1923, Donovan and Fallon renovated the commercial space at the corner of Monument and Main Streets, adding a decorative stained glass nameplate over the plate glass storefront windows and green marble cladding

FIGURE 44.2
The John Hurd House in 1972, prior to restorations (BLC 1972a; image courtesy of the City of Boston Archives).

to the windows' base. The pharmacy would remain the building's owner until 1964, though the upper apartments had become vacant by the 1930s, as Charlestown faced an economic decline in the mid-twentieth century. The arrival of the elevated railway on Main Street in 1899 greatly affected the value of the commercial and rental units along its route. Regardless, throughout the 1970s a pharmacy remained in the building after Donovan and Fallon left, but the building began to fall into disrepair (figure 44.2).[7]

In 1981, Historic Boston Incorporated purchased the Hurd House, and using funds that included grants from the Massachusetts Historical Commission, it was able both to make the repairs necessary to prevent the building from collapsing and to restore the exterior.[8] Charlestown residents purchased the property from HBI and completed the restoration of the apartments and commercial spaces in the building.[9] Fortunately, the early-twentieth-century Donovan and Fallon signage and exterior cladding, as well as much of the post-1868 exterior elements survived into the late twentieth century, which greatly aided the preservation efforts. The elevated railroad was removed during the Big Dig project, returning Main Street to its former open appearance.

The John Hurd House is on the National Register but is not a Boston Landmark. Its well-restored and -maintained exterior adds attractive commercial and residential space to the streetscape along Main Street, and the building currently houses a café and popular restaurant.

# 45. Memorial Hall

14 Green Street, Charlestown | 1791

FIGURE 45.1
View of Memorial
Hall with its
original gardens
around 1870
(BPL 1870; image
courtesy of the
BPL).

In 1791, Samuel Dexter purchased a one-acre lot from John Hay, a Charlestown farmer, just to the west of the main center of Charlestown, joining other wealthy Charlestown residents in building new mansions and estates after the 1775 fires.[1]

Dexter hired builders to construct a large mansion on the rear of his sloped lot, a location that increased the house's visibility and made room for a large formal garden in front of the home. The house has symmetrical five-bay facade with a Georgian hipped roof and chimneys placed at the outside of the roofline, similar to many other houses in this book but on a larger scale due to Dexter's wealth. The house became, and still is, one of the largest homes ever built in Charlestown. Dexter moved into the home with his wife, Catherine, and their son, Samuel William Dexter, was born there.

Soon after the move, Dexter's political career flourished. He was elected to the Massachusetts State Senate in 1792 and served as a representative in the US Congress in 1793–1795 and as a US senator in 1799–1800. In 1800, President John Adams appointed Dexter secretary of war, and he chose to sell his Charlestown home.[2]

Giles Alexander purchased the Dexter mansion in 1800. This Alexander's relationship to the Giles Alexander who funded the construction of the building on lot 60 on Long Wharf (see building #26) is unclear. In 1814, the house passed to the father of Nathaniel Bridge, and then to Bridge himself. From 1814 to 1830, Bridge used his wealth from his business on Central Wharf in Boston to improve the property. The well-traveled Bridge brought worldly design influences to the Dexter garden. He invested heavily in trained gardeners and worked to realize his vision of a manicured and stately garden including large trees of rare species, extensive espaliered fruit trees along the walls of the garden, and carefully executed hedges (figure 45.1).[3]

After Bridge's death in 1831, ownership of the house passed through multiple wealthy Charlestown residents until 1850, when the property was scheduled to be broken up into twelve smaller lots and sold at auction. Fortunately, Rhodes Lockwood purchased both the house and main garden lots, preserving both and avoiding their redevelopment.[4]

In 1887, the Abraham Lincoln Post Number 11 of the Grand Army of the Republic purchased the house, converting it into Memorial Hall. Part of this conversion included the lifting of the second floor's roofline to convert the floor into a hall for meetings and other events.[5] The post still owns and maintains the property, which has deteriorated over time.

The post's recent leaders worked with the Charlestown Preservation Society and Charlestown Historical Society to restore the property.[6] They have raised hundreds of thousands of dollars in grant funding to stabilize the house and begin its restoration, including a $500,000 grant in 2019 from Boston's Community Preservation Committee (CPC) to restore three sides of the building's exterior and improve accessibility at the property.[7] Though the historic significance of the building was made explicit when the CPC elected to partially fund the restorations, the property is not a Boston Landmark, nor is it on the National Register. This funding is critical to the restoration efforts of this historic property, but it is likely that a full restoration would cost more than $2 million.

# 46. Thompson House

9 Thompson Street, Charlestown | Ca. 1794

Timothy Thompson, a carpenter, married Mary Frothingham in January 1775, just months before the Revolution began. In April, the couple fled to Woburn when they heard of troops marching to Charlestown after the Battles of Lexington and Concord. The Thompsons lost their first home when the town of Charlestown burned during the Battle of Bunker Hill on June 17.[1]

When the couple returned after the Battle of Bunker Hill, they purchased a new building lot from Mary's father, and Timothy built a two-room structure containing a room for living and a shop for his carpentry business—which was growing as Charleston was rebuilt. In February 24, 1777, Timothy Thompson Jr. was born, the first boy born in Charlestown after the fire. In the same year, Thompson Sr. moved his two-room house to an adjacent lot on Back Lane (later Warren Street). There he expanded the building, converting it into a larger house, and he built a new house on his former lot (see building #47) (figure 46.1).[2]

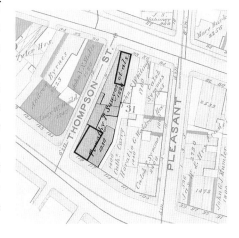

FIGURE 46.1
Map showing the association of the two Thompson houses (outlined in blue) discussed in this (the top building) and the following chapter (the bottom building) (G. W. Bromley and Co. 1892; image courtesy of the Norman B. Leventhal Map Center, edits by author).

It is possible that the house discussed in this chapter is the earlier ca. 1777 house that was moved to the location and expanded. If so, it is likely that portions of the house are part of the oldest building in Charlestown. A more conservative interpretation is that this is a slightly later home built on the spot around 1794, soon after Thompson sold the property to move into the new house he had just finished. This is partially supported by the idea that 9 Thompson Street is built with a brick party wall between itself and number 6, suggesting these two properties were developed in tandem as a double house. That would be less likely though not impossible if the 9 Thompson Street property had been moved there after already being partially built. A dendrochronological survey of the property might reveal whether the original timbers of the building date to the 1770s or the 1790s.

The building is currently a five-bay Georgian structure with three stories, a low hipped roof, and chimneys placed at the rear of the building and shared with the house at 6 Thompson Street. The property has been a single-family home for much of its existence. In the late 1800s, both 6 and 9 Thompson were owned by John S. Whiting, who married Lucy Loring Barker. They lived in the homes with their three children and a servant. In the twentieth century, number 6 Thompson either was torn down or burned. The current building in the spot is a 1973 rebuilding of the former Georgian-style house using new materials.

In the 1890s, Timothy Thompson Sawyer, a noted Charlestown historian and descendant of Timothy Thompson (who may have built the building), owned both this house and the neighboring c. 1794 Timothy Thompson House (see building #47). Sawyer was a banker and politician who served as mayor of Charlestown and as both a state representative and senator.[3] The house is not a Boston Landmark, nor is it on the National Register. Its significance comes from its association with the Thompson family and its location in a group of early-eighteen- and nineteenth-century buildings, including several in this book (buildings #31, #43–44, and #47), all of which are within a small area of Charlestown and which together represent one of the more intact concentrations of historic architecture in Boston.

While living in the adjacent lot (see building #46), Timothy Thompson built a new three-story home for his family. The rear of this new home currently faces Thompson Street, with the front entrance facing an open side yard and its narrow end facing Main Street. Architecturally, the house represents a transition between the Georgian and Federal styles, with the low hipped roof and quoins of the Georgian style and a shorter third story that is typical of a Federal house. It has a symmetrical five-bay front facade with a narrower two-bay side.[1]

The house remained in the Thompson family for decades. In the nineteenth century the house was occupied by Benjamin Thompson, who served in the US House of Representatives from 1848 to 1852. The first floor was used for commercial purposes, as was a small addition in the yard in front of the house, for much of the nineteenth century. The space was occupied by the apothecary shop of William B. Morse and later by a millinery store operated by Sarah Colby. Sarah's son, Gardner Colby, would eventually start his own store and become a wealthy businessman. In 1864, Colby gave $50,000 to a struggling Maine college—the first of several donations he made—which resulted in its renaming and revival as Colby College in 1867.[2]

The property passed to the Sawyer family when Susan Thompson married William Sawyer. Their son, Timothy Thompson Sawyer, lived in the house in the late nineteenth and early twentieth centuries. He was a businessman specializing in the global ice market, which brought refrigeration to the West Indies, Rio de Janeiro, and Kolkata (then Calcutta). After serving in the Massachusetts House of Representatives and then the state Senate, Sawyer spent his retirement as a prominent local historian and color commentator, writing *Old Charlestown*—which is cited extensively in this book.

At the end of the twentieth century, James Rivers Adams purchased the property (figure 47.1). A professional contractor, he had already restored the Warren Tavern (building #31) and Deacon John Larkin House (building #43), and he now focused on restoring his own property. Work began with a $305,000 restoration grant from the Boston Redevelopment Association. During the restoration, evidence emerged that the house's main entrance may once have faced Thompson Street.[3]

Adams moved the store to the southeast of the house, restoring the current garden space in front of the building, and then restored the first floor based on similar houses from the period (figure 47.2).[4] The original window cases were uncovered and the window frames reproduced from discarded examples found in the home.[5] During the restorations, the removal of a wall revealed a sealed door behind which was a sealed kitchen that included pots and a fireplace and that may have been closed off since the eighteenth century.[6] The property is not a Boston Landmark, nor is it listed on the National Register. Its sensitive restoration to its eighteenth-century appearance is well maintained by the current owners, who have kept this significant historic property in great condition.

FIGURE 47.2 View of the Timothy Thompson House after its renovation (BLC 1970a; image courtesy of the City of Boston Archives).

# 48. William Wiley House

45 Rutherford Avenue, Charlestown  |  Ca. 1794

Isaac Rand purchased the land that would become the William Wiley House from John Newell in 1741. In 1790—after any structures on the property had been burned during the Battle of Bunker Hill—it passed to his daughter, Margaret, and her husband, Nathaniel Austin, a pewterer.[1] Isaac Rand's probate does not mention any buildings on the land, which suggests that the property was undeveloped at this point.[2]

In 1794, the Austins sold the property to William Wiley, a carpenter, who probably built the house soon afterward using popular eighteenth-century pattern books, given its textbook Georgian style and proportions. Wiley's house faces south and is five bays wide by two bays deep. It has a central front door and an unusual hipped roof with a gambrel-like smaller hipped roof on top of it (referred to as a hip-on-hip roof).[3]

Wiley was originally from Reading, Massachusetts, a descendant of one of the town's early settlers.[4] He moved to Charlestown in 1786, probably due to the bustling house-building industry that resulted from the hundreds of residents who were attempting to rebuild homes at the same time. In 1807, Wiley sold the house to his brother, John, who owned of the property until his death in 1833.[5]

FIGURE 48.1
Map of the William Wiley House (outlined in red) in 1912, with encroaching brick and wood buildings (G. W. Bromley and Co. 1912; image courtesy of the Norman B. Leventhal Map Center, edits by author).

John left the property to Hannah Wiley, his niece and William's daughter. In 1832 Hannah had married her cousin, Peter Brown Wiley, and the property remained Hannah's until her death in 1871.[6]

The property then moved rapidly through several owners. Around 1870, the house was enlarged with a two-story addition on its eastern side. This is unusual, as it extends forward, in front of the house. For the remaining century, the property included both the main historic house and a row of brick buildings facing Washington Street. With other buildings rising along Rutherford Avenue in front of the house (figure 48.1), the eighteenth-century wooden Wiley house became, functionally, a detached apartment behind the row houses, which probably helped it remain standing: the density of new buildings met the needs of the growing town, and demolition of the older house was avoided.[7]

After surviving the economic slump of Boston in the first half of the twentieth century, the building underwent a revival. At the end of that century, the wooden buildings that were built in front of the house and obscured its entrance were demolished, creating valuable off-street parking for the Wiley House owners. The property lost at least one of its chimneys at some point, and the remaining chimney's height was increased so as not to pose a risk to the nearby taller brick buildings. In 1986 and 1987, the owners of the house had it extensively renovated to its current and well-maintained appearance, including completely rebuilding the original and rare hip-on-hip roof.[8] The house is not a Boston Landmark, nor is it on the National Register.

# 49. Daniel Carter House

19 Putnam Street, Charlestown | Ca. 1794

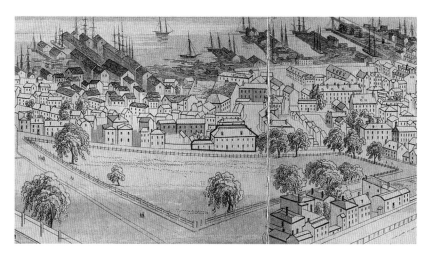

FIGURE 49.1 Panorama of Common Street and the Charlestown Training Field drawn in 1848, showing the Salem Turnpike Hotel and Carter House (outlined in red) as one continuous building with two entrances (Mallory and Millie 1848; image courtesy of the BPL, edits by author).

Daniel Carter purchased a lot of open land from Aaron Putnam in late 1794.[1] The lot was across the street from the town training field, where the local militia trained before and after the Revolution.

Carter was a carpenter, and it is highly likely that he immediately set about building the structure currently on the site.[2] He built a large late Georgian house with five bays along Putnam Street, with a hipped roof of the period and central doorway that was much altered later. On the Common Street side, the property probably had an identical five-bay facade, making it a large L-shape property on a prominent corner in town.

Thomas Robbins purchased the property from John Carter, Daniel's son, in 1804. Robbins, described as an "inn holder" in the 1804 deed, probably converted the property into an inn at this time.[3] In 1802, the Salem Turnpike had reached Charlestown and passed by the house, ending in the nearby City Square. The many travelers it brought probably attracted Robbins's attention. The neighboring property, an extension of this house (see building #50 for more discussion and images), was the primary Salem Turnpike Hotel, so Robbins may have lived in part of the Putnam Street property and run the attached hotel, or the entire combined properties may have functioned as a hotel.[4]

By the mid-nineteenth century, the two properties had separate ownership and functions, though an 1848 drawing of the view from the newly constructed Bunker Hill Monument illustrates this building and the Salem Turnpike

Hotel as one continuous building nearly a block long. This suggests that the two were still experienced as one structure in the late 1840s (figure 49.1). After the house had passed through multiple owners, James Deblois sold it in 1852 to James Sutton, referred to in documents variably as a cabinet, pump, or block maker at the nearby Charlestown Navy Yard.[5]

The Navy Yard began in 1800 as a shipbuilding facility for the newly created US Navy, and by the mid-nineteenth century it had become a massive operation, attracting well-paid builders and specialists who lived in the nearby homes a short walk away. The 1850 census from two years prior to his purchase included James Sutton; his wife, Charlotte; and their two children, John and Mary. To supplement his income, James and Charlotte took in boarders, including the four other families listed in the 1855 state census.[6] By 1860, their financial position seems to have improved, and that year's federal census records the couple as living in the home with their servant, Emily, and a seven-year-old named Ella Smith—all listed together as a single-family unit.[7]

The property remained in the hands of the Suttons until the family sold it to William Long in 1879.[8] Throughout the twentieth century, the property remained remarkably intact and unchanged, as Charlestown became home to a diverse community of New Englanders and immigrants. The Daniel Carter House is not listed on the National Register, nor is it a Boston Landmark.

# 50. Salem Turnpike Hotel

16 Common Street, Charlestown  |  Ca. 1794

Despite its current appearance, a significant portion of this building belongs to the Daniel Carter House (see building #49), to which it is attached. When Carter built his home around 1794, it was a building five bays deep by five bays wide that hooked around the corner of Putnam and Common Streets, probably with an entrance in the center of both street facades (figure 50.1).

In 1804, Thomas Robbins, an inn holder, purchased the Carter House, later expanding the property as the demand for lodging increased.[1] This expansion appears to have occurred in 1805, when Josiah Gurney purchased the adjacent lot to the northeast of the Carter House on Common Street. Gurney, a shipbuilder, was probably responsible for building the addition to the property himself. Though it is this addition and the portions of the building that were incorporated from the Carter House that have been historically known as the Salem Turnpike Hotel, it is not entirely clear if Gurney operated the hotel independently from Robbins or if—as seems more likely—Gurney and Robbins were business partners. The building remained a hotel for only a short time, though it has retained its historic name.[2]

In 1810, Matthew Rice purchased the house, and his family remained its owners through the early 1900s. Rice was a significant member of the Charlestown community, as the foreman of the joiners' department at the Charlestown Navy Yard (see building #49). There, he led significant projects—including the finishing and framing of multiple buildings in the Navy Yard, including the Landmark-designated 1834 Charlestown Navy Yard Ropewalk. Most significantly, he was responsible for repairs to the USS *Constitution*, which saw combat throughout the early nineteenth century and returned to the Charlestown Navy Yard for repairs.[3]

In the 1820 census, Matthew Rice was listed with his wife, Sally; and six children, including two boys and two girls younger than ten and two other girls younger than sixteen.[4] The Rice family would remain owners and occupiers of the property through the early twentieth century.

FIGURE 50.1
Views of the Salem Turnpike Hotel (left) and Daniel Carter House (right) as they appear today (top) and as they would appear if the Carter House had retained its original northern facade and entrance (bottom) (photo and edits by author).

Like the adjoining Carter House, the Salem Turnpike Hotel survived the nineteenth and twentieth centuries in remarkably good condition, without any significant changes. Though this rare building from the eighteenth is not a Boston Landmark or listed on the National Register, it is a significant historic place in Massachusetts, both because it served as a hotel to travelers and because of its association with Matthew Rice.

# Conclusion. Honorable Mentions

Following the first printing of this book in 2021, researchers have determined the following buildings are some of Boston's oldest.

## 42-44 Shirley Street

Roxbury | Ca. 1750

Research in 2019 revealed this building to be one half of a former stable built for Governor William Shirley (see building #19). The building's primary function was to house Shirley's horses, though it is possible if not likely that enslaved people also lived in the building on the second floor. In 2021 both the Shirley-Eustis House and 42-44 Shirley Street were formally designated protected Boston Landmarks. In 2023, the Shirley Eustis Association purchased 42-44 Shirley Street with funding in part provided by a Community Preservation Commission grant.

FIGURE C.1
The 42-44 Shirley Street house (Bagley 2016; photo by author).

## John Capen House

681 River Street, Mattapan | Ca. 1782

When this book was first printed, the John Capen House was listed as a potential oldest house based on the purchase of 36 acres of land surrounding the building in 1781 and a later document in 1829. This large gap between documents made it impossible to accurately estimate the building's construction date on the large parcel. In 2022, Marti Glynn, a researcher for the Dorchester Historical Society working on behalf of the building's current owner, identified a 1786 mortgage on the property that mentions a house and barn. From this early date and the building's architecture, it seems likely that the current house is the same one mentioned in the mortgage and Capen had the house built soon after his purchase of the land. Today the house is privately owned.

FIGURE C.2
The John Capen House (Bagley 2016; photo by author).

Numerous buildings may be old enough to be included in this book, but additional data are needed to confirm their age. They include:

8 Brewer Street, Jamaica Plain
(possibly the 1711 Sally Brewer House)

991 and 1011 Centre Street, Jamaica Plain
(possibly built in the late eighteenth century)

1070–72 Washington Street, Dorchester
(built between 1788 and 1796)

Ozias Goodwin House, 7 Jackson Avenue, North End
(ca. 1795)

The following built structures also qualify for honorable mention status because they are old enough to be included in this book, but they did not meet the technical requirements of a Boston building (explained in the introduction).

FIGURE C.3 Reconstructed fishweirs by the Boston artist Ross Miller, installed annually each spring during the herring run by local schoolchildren and Native people (Bagley 2016; photo by author).

## Back Bay Fishweirs

Back Bay | Ca. 3200 BCE

The Back Bay Fishweirs constitute one of the largest structures ever built in Boston, spanning multiple acres under thirty feet of fill in Back Bay. Built between 3,600 and 5,200 years ago, these Massachuset Native creations consist of wooden fence-like structures used to corral and capture spawning herring and alewives in the spring. The fishweirs were not included in this book as they do not have a roof and are not visible. Nonetheless, they deserve recognition here as the oldest structure built by people in Boston, and one of the oldest and largest Native structures ever built.

## Barnard Capen House

In storage | Ca. 1637

Portions of the Barnard Capen House may have been built before 1637, which would make it one of the oldest houses in the United States. It stood on Washington Street until new construction threatened it with demolition. In 1909, Kenneth Grant Tremayne Webster, a Harvard professor, paid to have the property dismantled and rebuilt at 427 Hillside Street in Milton, Massachusetts. It remained until 2006, when the property was sold. The house was dismantled again and put into storage, where it remains. If it were to be reassembled somewhere in Boston, it could become the oldest house in Boston. It does not qualify for this book as its elements are not currently arranged in their approximate original appearance.

## Deane Winthrop House

34 Shirley Street, Winthrop | Ca. 1675

In 1632, Boston annexed the place that we now call Winthrop. Around 1675, Deane Winthrop—the sixth son of John Winthrop, the first governor of the Massachusetts Bay Colony—paid to have this building made. At the time of its construction, it was in the town of Boston, and if that were still the case today, it would be the second oldest building in the city. However, in 1739, Chelsea, Revere, and Winthrop withdrew from the town of Boston. Thus, the building does not qualify for this book.

## Third Church Parsonage

60 McBride Street, Jamaica Plain | Before 1760

Prior to the building of the Loring Greenough House (see building #24), this
property contained the parsonage for the Third Church in Roxbury, which
would later become Jamaica Plain. In 1760, the year when construction of the
Loring house began, Benjamin Pemberton purchased the parsonage and had
it moved to the corner of Centre and Monument Streets. In 1851, the property
was sold and the parsonage was moved—first to South Street and later east
down Keyes Street (now McBride), where it is believed that it currently resides at 60 McBride Street (figure C.5). The property seen in the illustration
here has changed so radically that it is possible that this is not the building
that was moved four times. Further evidence would be needed to determine
if this building is one of the fifty oldest buildings in Boston.

## USS *Constitution*

Charlestown Navy Yard, Dry Dock 1 | 1794

The keel of the ship affectionately known as Old
Ironsides was laid down on November 1, 1794,
at a shipyard located near the present US Coast
Guard base in the North End. The USS *Constitu-*
*tion* is not included in the main text of this book
because it is not a land-based structure.

FIGURE C.8 The USS *Constitution* as seen
in 1970 (BLC 1970c; image courtesy of the
City of Boston Archives).

# Parting Thoughts

The buildings included in this book represent not only Boston's early history, but also the ongoing legacy of the oldest places in the city. These buildings continue to provide housing, work spaces, educational opportunities, recreation, and protection for Boston's residents and visitors. They also contribute greatly to attracting the historic tourists on whom much of Boston's economy relies.

The future is brighter than ever for historic preservation efforts, since Bostonians voted to adopt the statewide Community Preservation Act in 2016. This created the Community Preservation Commission and funded it with millions of annual tax dollars to be devoted to historic preservation projects in Boston. Still, the risk to historic buildings is also greater than ever, as Boston grows.

Preservation efforts matter. The fifty buildings listed in this book represent a wide spectrum of preservation efforts, from nonprofits dedicated solely to the protection of a single building to neglect. I hope that this book and the stories in it spark genuine interest and involvement in preservation efforts that can protect these buildings and the many other old buildings in Boston that could not be included here.

Some of the fifty properties are in the National Register or are National Historic Landmarks, but these designations provide few legal protections to these buildings unless the work done to them triggers state and federal historic preservation laws—a relatively rare event.

Designating these buildings Boston Landmarks is the most powerful tool for preserving them from inappropriate changes and loss. Community support is necessary for the Landmarking process to occur. If the BLC considers any of these buildings for Landmark status, Boston residents can support their preservation by making their voices and opinions heard at the BLC hearings. In addition, there are many opportunities for nonresident readers to get involved in their own communities to support the preservation of the historic places near them.

# Notes

INTRODUCTION

1. Boston Maps 2019.
2. Suffolk County, *Suffolk Registry of Deeds* (SRD), 51:117.
3. Suffolk County, *Suffolk County Massachusetts Probate Records* (SCMPR), case no. 16409 [16409].
4. SCMPR, 13484.
5. Osgood 1873, 341.
6. Guarino 2011, 78; Osgood 1873, 342.
7. Floyd 1979.
8. Burdett 1877, 88–89.
9. Burdett 1877, 89.
10. Massachusetts Historical Commission (MHC) 1980c.
11. Campbell 1974.
12. Sammarco 2017, 93.

1. BLAKE HOUSE

1. Dorchester Historical Society (DHS) 1960, 9.
2. Boston Landmarks Commission (BLC) 1977b, 15.
3. MHC 2007a, 3.
4. DHS 1960, 9.
5. DHS 1960, 9.
6. Zimmer 1974; Poulsen 2011.
7. Zimmer 1974.
8. Historic Preservation and Design 2007.
9. Miles and Worthington 2007.

2. PAUL REVERE HOUSE

1. Roper 1974.
2. Roper 1974.
3. Heitert et al. 2014, 18.
4. National Park Service (NPS) 1975, 3.
5. NPS 1975, 3.

6. Heitert et al. 2014, 20–21.
7. NPS 1975, 3
8. United States Census Bureau 1883, 450.
9. Heitert et al. 2014, 21.
10. Heitert et al. 2014, 21.
11. NPS 1975, 3.
12. "Restoration of the Paul Revere House, Boston" 1914, 80.
13. "Restoration of the Paul Revere House, Boston" 1914, 80.
14. MHC 1987b, 4.

3. PIERCE HOUSE

1. NPS 2009, 3.
2. Miles et al. 2002.
3. NPS 2009, 3.
4. NPS 2009, 2.
5. NPS 2009, 3.
6. NPS 2009, 3 and 5.
7. NPS 2009, 3.
8. NPS 2009, 2.
9. NPS 2009, 2.
10. NPS 2009, 5.
11. NPS 2009, 2.

4. LEMUEL CLAP HOUSE

1. DHS 1960, 11.
2. DHS 1960.
3. DHS 1960, 12.
4. DHS 1960, 13.
5. DHS 1960, 13.
6. DHS 1960, 13.
7. DHS 1960, 13.

5. PIERCE-HICHBORN HOUSE

1. MHC 1989b, 4.
2. Detwiller 1976, 2.

3. MHC 1989b, 4.

4. SRD, 25:154.

5. MHC 1989b, 4.

6. MHC 1989b, 4.

7. Detwiller 1976, 23–24.

8. United States Census Bureau 1900.

9. MHC 1989b, 4.

10. MHC 1989b, 4.

## 6. EBENEZER CLOUGH HOUSE

1. Bagley et al. 2017, 15.

2. Bagley et al. 2017, 15.

3. MHC 1990.

4. Bagley et al. 2017, 15.

5. Bagley et al. 2017, 15.

6. Bagley et al. 2017, 15.

7. Bagley et al. 2017, 16.

8. Bagley et al. 2017, 16.

9. Nylander et al. 1986, 87.

10. A. Webster 2016, 14.

11. A. Webster 2016, 42.

## 7. OLD STATE HOUSE

1. MHC 2007c.

2. MHC 2007c, 4.

3. MHC 2007c, 4.

4. BLC 1994, 7.

5. BLC 1994, 7 and 9.

6. BLC 1994, 16.

7. BLC 1994, 16.

8. BLC 1994, 16.

9. BLC 1994, 12.

10. BLC 1994.

11. BLC 1994.

12. BLC 1994.

13. BLC 1994.

## 8. BOSTON LIGHT STATION

1. MHC 1981.

2. MHC 1981.

3. MHC 1981.

4. MHC 1981.

5. MHC 1981.

6. MHC 1981.

7. MHC 1981.

8. MHC 1981.

9. MHC 1981.

10. Snowman and Thomson 2016.

11. Snowman and Thomson 2016.

12. Associated Press 2020.

## 9. UNION OYSTER HOUSE

1. MHC 2007d.

2. MHC 2007d.

3. MHC 2007d.

4. Quoted in SRD, 32:65.
See also MHC 2007d, 3.

5. MHC 2007d.

6. MHC 2007d.

7. MHC 2007d.

## 10. EBENEZER SMITH HOUSE

1. MHC 1978b, 3.

2. MHC 1978b, 3.

3. Winship 1902, 31.

4. Winship 1902, 32–33.

5. Winship 1902, 32.

6. Winship 1902, 33.

7. Marchione 1998–2001.

8. MHC 1978b, 3.

9. MHC 1978c, 3.

## 11. KIMBALL-CHEEVER HOUSE

1. SRD, 31:95.

2. Quoted in SRD, 61:166 and 74:171.

3. SRD, 61:166 and 74:171.

4. Hassam 1884, 178.

5. SCMPR, 9898, inventory.

6. City of Boston (COB) 1899, 255.

7. SCMPR, 9898, will.

## 12. OLD CORNER BOOKSTORE

1. MHC 2000, 4.

2. MHC 2000, 4.

3. MHC 2000, 4–5.

4. Library of Congress 1999.

5. MHC 2000, 5.

6. MHC 2000, 5.

7. MHC 2000, 5.

13. OLD NORTH CHURCH

1. Todd 2020.

2. NPS 1969, 8.

3. NPS 1969, 8.

4. NPS 1969, 8.

5. NPS 1969, 8.

6. NPS 1969, 8.

7. NPS 1969, 9.

14. DANIELS-GOLDSMITH HOUSE

1. MHC 1978a.

2. MHC 1978a.

3. SRD, 1771:225.

4. MHC 1978a.

15. ANDREW CUNNINGHAM HOUSE

1. Cunningham, 1901.

2. MHC 2000, 4.

3. MHC 1980a.

4. MHC 1980a.

16. OLD SOUTH MEETING HOUSE

1. MHC 1980c, 4.

2. MHC 1980c, 4; H. Hill 1890.

3. H. Hill 1890, 438.

4. WBUR 2012.

5. MHC 1980c, 4.

6. MHC 1980b.

17. GRANT HOUSE

1. MHC 1987a.

2. SRD, 49:8.

3. SCMPR, 16002.

4. SRD, 181:251.

5. SRD, 190:280.

6. Weekly News-Letter 1730.

18. FANEUIL HALL

1. BLC 1987.

2. BLC 1987.

3. BLC 1987.

4. BLC 1987.

5. BLC 1987.

6. BLC 1987.

7. BLC 1987.

19. SHIRLEY-EUSTIS HOUSE

1. Detwiller 1979, 24.

2. NPS 1977.

3. Detwiller 1979.

4. NPS 1977.

5. NPS 1977; Detwiller 1979.

6. NRD 355–356.

7. Wright 1871, 171–72; Byrne et al 1899, 194–95.

8. SRD, 3,764:291–5.

20. THOMAS GARDNER HOUSE

1. MHC 1978b.

2. MHC 1978b.

3. MHC 1978b.

21. KING'S CHAPEL

1. MHC 2007b, 4.

2. Quoted in Jenks 1886, 86.

3. Greenwood 1833, 118.

4. Greenwood 1833, 125.

5. MHC 2007b, 5.

22. DILLAWAY-THOMAS HOUSE

1. Quoted in Ritchie and Miller 1994, 57.

2. Quoted in Ritchie and Miller 1994, 57; see also MHC 1973 4.

3. MHC 1973, 4.

4. Ritchie and Miller 1994, 57.

5. Ritchie and Miller 1994, 65.

6. Ritchie and Miller 1994, 65.

7. Ritchie and Miller 1994.

8. Ritchie and Miller 1994.

## 23. LINDEN HALL

1. MHC 1983, 3.
2. MHC 1983, 3.
3. Colonial Society of Massachusetts 1920, 14.
4. MHC 1983, 5.
5. MHC 1983, 5.
6. MHC 1983, 5.
7. MHC 1983, 5.
8. MHC 1983, 3.

## 24. LORING GREENOUGH HOUSE

1. MHC 1999, 13.
2. MHC 1999, 4.
3. MHC 1999, 4.
4. MHC 1999, 4.
5. MHC 1999, 4.
6. MHC 1999, 4.
7. Andrew Hatcher, personal communication during a 2019 tour of the house.
8. Hatcher, personal communication.
9. Hatcher, personal communication.

## 25. BENJAMIN FANEUIL GATEKEEPER HOUSE

1. Quoted in Brown 1900, 25; see also 16–18 and 25.
2. Brown 1900, 109–13.
3. MRD 58:373.
4. Brown 1900, 118–20.
5. Brown 1900, 118–20.
6. Brown 1900, 118–20.

## 26. GARDINER BUILDING

1. NPS 1991.
2. NPS 1991.
3. NPS 1991.
4. SRD, 219:127.
5. NPS 1991.
6. SRD, 411:245 and 654:38; SCMPR, 31986.
7. NPS 1991.

## 27. EBENEZER HANCOCK HOUSE

1. MHC 1989a, 3.
2. BLC 1977a.
3. MHC 1989a, 3; BLC 1977a.
4. MHC 1989a, 4; BLC 1977a.
5. MHC 1989a, 4; BLC 1977a.
6. MHC 1989a, 3; BLC 1977a.

## 28. CHARLES TILESTON HOUSE

1. SCMPR. 14767, will.
2. National Archives and Records Administration 1976.
3. SCMPR, 19057, inventory.
4. SRD, 163:107.
5. United States Census Bureau 1800.
6. NRD 186:190.

## 29. JOSEPH ROYALL HOUSE

1. Harris 1885, 352; Jackson 1907, 13.
2. Harris 1885, 354.
3. Harris 1885, 356.
4. Harris 1885, 354.
5. SRD, 144:125.
6. SRD, 144:126.
7. SRD, 147:43.
8. NRD, 6:49.
9. NRD, 39:171.
10. NRD, 354–61.
11. G.W. Bromley & Co. 1904

## 30. CLAPP-FIELD HOUSE

1. SRD, 121:206.
2. NRD, 72:97 and 73:146.
3. NRD, 116–98.
4. MHC 1995.
5. Historic Boston Incorporated 2011.

## 31. WARREN TAVERN

1. Quoted in Frothingham 1875, 127.
2. Leach 1780.
3. MHC 1987c; Bell 2011.
4. MHC 1987c.
5. MHC 1987c.

6. MHC 1987c.

7. MHC 1987c.

## 32. SPOONER-LAMBERT HOUSE

1. Drake 1905, 361.

2. Drake 1905, 361.

3. Bagwell Perez 1980.

4. Historic Boston Incorporated 2010.

5. Historic Boston Incorporated 2010.

## 33. BICKNELL HOUSE

1. City Council of Boston 1895.

2. COB 1910, 316.

3. NRD, 35:146.

4. McGlenen 1899, 54.

## 34. GLAPION-MIDDLETON HOUSE

1. Lanning 2005, 84.

2. Chamberlain 1925.

3. Chamberlain 1925.

4. Chamberlain 1925.

5. Chamberlain 1925.

6. Chamberlain 1925.

7. Quoted in Nell 1855, 27. See also Lanning 2005, 84.

8. History Project 1999.

9. Quoted in Chamberlain 1925, 225.

10. Chamberlain 1925.

## 35. FOWLER-CLARK-EPSTEIN FARM

1. BLC 2005.

2. BLC 2005.

3. BLC 2005.

4. Historic Boston Incorporated 2015a.

## 36. ELIJAH JONES HOUSE

1. SRD, 158:251.

2. SRD, 158:140.

3. SRD, 158:140; SCMPR, 27092.

4. SCMPR, 27092.

5. McNamee 2013, 147.

6. SCMPR, 27092; NRD 72:25.

7. NCMPR, 7520.

8. NRD 83:149; American Series of Popular Biographies 1901, 365.

9. NRD 177:2.

10. NRD 177:2.

11. American Antiquarian Society 2010; NRD 293:228.

12. SRD, 3,197:147.

## 37. GEORGE HAYNES HOUSE

1. NRD 20:255.

2. American Series of Popular Biographies 1901, 693.

3. NRD 23:94.

4. Clapp 1876, 226.

5. Clapp 1876, 226.

6. NRD 50:62.

7. NRD 48:171.

8. NRD 70:249.

9. Orcutt 1893, 447.

10. Orcutt 1893, 448.

11. NRD 110:77.

## 38. BRIGHTON FIRST CHURCH PARSONAGE

1. Marchione 1998–2001.

2. Foster 1797. A coquette is a term for a flirtatious woman.

3. Marchione 1998–2001.

4. Marchione 1998–2001.

## 39. BOND-GLOVER HOUSE

1. SRD, 159:143.

2. COB 1890, 226.

3. NRD 11:224.

4. NRD 44:43 and 35:130.

5. NRD 82:271 and 272.

6. Holden 1897.

7. Holden 1897.

8. Holden 1897.

9. Holden 1897.

10. Cocks and Cocks 1995, 49.

11. NRD 114:295.

**40. KILTON-BEAL HOUSE**

1. NRD 83:188.

**41. CALVIN BIRD HOUSE**

1. NRD 75:256.
2. Commonwealth of Massachusetts 1850.
3. G. W. Bromley and Co. 1894; Massachusetts Vital Records 1915.
4. G.W. Bromley and Co. 1904 and 1918.

**42. CAROLINE CAPEN HOUSE**

1. NCMPR, 3216
2. Commonwealth of Massachusetts 1915.
3. G.W. Bromley and Co. 1884 and 1889.
4. SCMPR, 89761.
5. G.W. Bromley and Co. 1918.

**43. DEACON JOHN LARKIN HOUSE**

1. Whittier 1907, 23.
2. MRD 83:446.
3. MCMPR, 13617.
4. MRD 1138:52.

**44. JOHN HURD HOUSE**

1. NPS 1985.
2. NPS 1985.
3. NPS 1985.
4. NPS 1985.
5. NPS 1985.
6. NPS 1985.
7. NPS 1985.
8. HBI 2017.
9. HBI 2017.

**45. MEMORIAL HALL**

1. Sawyer 1902, 17–23.
2. Sawyer 1902, 17–23.
3. Sawyer 1902, 17–23.
4. Sawyer 1902, 17–23.
5. Sawyer 1902, 17–23.
6. Daniel 2017.
7. Daniel 2019.

**46. THOMPSON HOUSE**

1. Sawyer 1902, 47–55.
2. Sawyer 1902, 47–55.
3. New England Historical and Geneaological Society 1906.

**47. TIMOTHY THOMPSON HOUSE**

1. MHC 1986.
2. Sawyer 1902, 47–55; Colby College 2013.
3. MHC 1986.
4. MHC 1986.
5. MHC 1986.
6. MHC 1986.

**48. WILLIAM WILEY HOUSE**

1. Sawyer 1902, 217.
2. MHC 1987d.
3. MHC 1987d.
4. Kueny 2019.
5. MHC 1987d.
6. MHC 1987d.
7. MHC 1987d.
8. MHC 1987d.

**49. DANIEL CARTER HOUSE**

1. MRD 118:201. .
2. MHC 1988.
3. Quoted in MHC 1988, 3.
4. MHC 1988.
5. SRD, 591:150.
6. Commonwealth of Massachusetts 1855.
7. United States Census Bureau 1860.
8. SRD, 911:413–14.

**50. SALEM TURNPIKE HOTEL**

1. MHC 1988.
2. MHC 1988.
3. MHC 1988.
4. United States Census Bureau 1820.

# Bibliography

Abdalian, Leon H.

    1920a   *Front View Deane Winthrop House, Winthrop, Mass.* Leon Abdalian Collection, Boston Public Library Print Department, Boston, MA.

    1920b   *Old Corner Bookstore, Boston, MA.* Leon Abdalian Collection, Boston Public Library Print Department, Boston MA.

American Antiquarian Society

    2010   "Tileston and Hollingsworth, Papers, 1755–1963: Sources of Information on Collection." American Antiquarian Society. https://www.americanantiquarian.org/Findingaids/tileston_and_hollingsworth.pdf, Revised March 5.

American Series of Popular Biographies

    1901   *Massachusetts Edition: Biographical Sketches of Representative Citizens of the Commonwealth of Massachusetts.* Graves and Steinbarger, Boston, MA.

Associated Press

    2020   "Coast Guard Seeks New Steward for Historic Boston Lighthouse." military.com /daily-news/2020/05/18/coast-guard-seeks -new-steward-historic-boston-lighthouse .html. May 18.

Bagley, Joseph

    2016   *A History of Boston in 50 Artifacts.* University Press of New England, Hanover, NH.

Bagley, Joseph, Alexandra Crowder, and Andrew Webster

    2017   "Archaeological Site Examination of the Clough House Backlot, 21 Unity Street, Christ (Old North) Church Campus, North End, Boston, Massachusetts." Boston City Archaeology Program. On file at the Massachusetts Historical Commission, Boston, MA.

Bagwell Perez, Madeline

    1980   Ladies Unity Club (Boston, Mass.). Records of the Ladies Unity Club, 1904–1951: A Finding Aid. Arthur and Elizabeth Schlesinger Library on the History of Women in America. Schlesinger Library, Radcliffe Institute, Cambridge, MA https://hollisarchives.lib.harvard .edu/repositories/8/resources/5466, accessed on July 29, 2020.

Bell, J. L.

    2011   "The Boston Tea Party's Mysterious 'E.N.'" Boston 1775. http://boston1775.blogspot.com /2011/12/boston-tea-partys-mysterious-en .html. December 15.

Black, James W.

    1875   *Old State House.* Boston Public Library Arts Department, Boston, MA.

    1876   *Old South.* Boston Public Library Arts Department, Boston, MA.

Boston Landmarks Commission (BLC)

    1875 [ca.]   *Centre Street at Pond Street, Linden Hall.* BLC image collection, Collection 5210.004, City of Boston Archives, Boston, MA.

    1970a   *9 Thompson Street, Timothy Thompson House.* BLC image collection, Collection 5210.004, City of Boston Archives, Boston, MA.

    1970b   *105 Main Street, 2 Pleasant Street, Warren Tavern "Thompson Triangle."* BLC image collection, Collection 5210.004, City of Boston Archives, Boston, MA.

    1970c   *Charlestown Navy Yard, USS Constitution.* BLC image collection, Collection 5210.004, City of Boston Archives, Boston, MA.

    1972a   *John Larkin House, 55–61 Main Street.* BLC image collection, Collection 5210.004, City of Boston Archives, Boston, MA.

1972b   *John Larkin House, Rear, Main Street.*
BLC image collection, Collection 5210.004,
City of Boston Archives, Boston, MA.

1975   *Unknown Location in Dorchester.*
BLC image collection, Dorchester Series,
Collection 5210.004, City of Boston Archives,
Boston, MA.

1977a   "Ebenezer Hancock House." BLC Study
Report, Boston, MA.

1977b   "James Blake House." BLC Study Report,
Boston, MA.

1981   *John Eliot Square, Dillaway-Thomas House
with Byron Rushing.* BLC image collection,
Collection 5210.004, City of Boston Archives,
Boston, MA.

1987   "Faneuil Hall." BLC Study Report,
Boston, MA.

1994   "Old State House." BLC Study Report,
Boston, MA.

2005   "Fowler-Clark Farm." BLC Study Report,
Boston, MA.

Boston Maps

2019   "Boston Buildings." https://data.boston
.gov/dataset/boston-buildings. Accessed
July 29, 2020. City of Boston, Boston, MA.

Boston Planning and Development Agency

2019   "Boston Streets and Neighborhoods."
http://www.bostonplans.org/getattachment
/69165a09-db81-4145-9833-b36a4ce43cc5/.
Accessed August 17, 2020. City of Boston,
Boston, MA.

Boston Public Library (BPL)

1835 [ca.]   *Boston, Massachusetts. Hancock House.*
BPL Arts Department, Boston, MA.

1845 [ca.]   *Christ Church, Boston. Erected
A.D. 1723.* J. H. Bufford and Co. BPL Arts
Department, Boston, MA.

1860a [ca.]   *Christ Church, Salem St., Boston.
Interior.* BPL Arts Department, Boston, MA.

1860b [ca.]   *Old Feather Store. Cor. Ann and
Market Sts., 1680–1860.* BPL Arts Department,
Boston, MA.

1860c [ca.]   *Old House on Union St. Built prior to*

1769. *Scene of Count Rumford's Clerkship.* BPL
Arts Department, Boston, MA.

1870 [ca.]   *Dexter House.* BPL Arts Department,
Boston, MA.

1880a [ca.]   *Boston, Massachusetts, Old South
Church. Interior.* BPL Arts Department,
Boston, MA.

1880b [ca.]   *Faneuil Hall, Boston.* BPL Print
Department, Boston, MA.

1880c [ca.]   *King's Chapel, Interior.* BPL Print
Department, Boston, MA.

1890 [ca.]   *Blake House, Dorchester.* BPL Arts
Department, Boston, MA.

1898a [ca.]   *Loring-Greenough House, Jamaica
Plain.* BPL Arts Department, Boston, MA.

1898b [ca.]   *The Marshall House, Marshall Street.*
BPL Arts Department, Boston, MA.

1898c [ca.]   *Paul Revere House, North
Square, North End.* BPL Arts Department,
Boston, MA.

1898d [ca.]   *The Pierce House, Oak Avenue
in Dorchester.* BPL Arts Department,
Boston, MA.

1898e [ca.]   *Roger Clapp House, Dorchester.*
BPL Arts Department, Boston, MA.

1898f [ca.]   *Unity Street in the North End.*
BPL Arts Department, Boston, MA.

1900a [ca.]   *Boston, Cotton Mather House,
Hanover St., 1677.* BPL Arts Department,
Boston, MA.

1900b [ca.]   *The Old South Stands.* BPL Arts
Department, Boston, MA.

1920 [ca.]   *Union Oyster House, Union
Street, Estab. 1826.* BPL Arts Department,
Boston, MA.

Brighton-Allston Historical Society

1900a [ca.]   *Faneuil Estate.* Brighton-Allston
Historical Society, Boston, MA.

1900b [ca.]   *Gardiner House.* Brighton-Allston
Historical Society, Boston, MA.

1920 [ca.]   *Faneuil St. Gatekeeper's House.*
Brighton-Allston Historical Society,
Boston, MA.

Brown, Abram English
1900   *Faneuil Hall and Faneuil Hall Market*. Lee and Shehard, Boston, MA.

Burgis, William
1730 [ca.]   *To the Merchants of Boston This View of the Light House Is Most Humbly Presented by Their Humble Servt. Wm. Burgis*. Boston Public Library Arts Department, Boston, MA.

Byrne, Very Rev. William, William Leahy, Rev. John McCoy, Rev. James O'Donnell, Rev. Andrew Dowling, Rev. John Finen, Edmund Young, and Rt. Rev. John Michaud
1899   *History of the Catholic Church in the New England States*. Vol. 1. Hurd and Everts Co., Boston, MA.

Burdett, Edward Watson
1877   *History of the Old South Meeting-House in Boston*. B. B. Russell, Boston, MA.

Campbell, Robert
1974   "70 Cities Protect Landmarks, but Boston Isn't One of Them." *Boston Globe*, May 19.

Carmack, David
2010 [ca.]   *Boards, Pierce House, Dorchester, Mass*. PC006: Properties Photographic Collection, Historic New England, Boston, MA.

Chamberlain, Allen
1925   *Beacon Hill: Its Ancient Pastures and Early Mansions*. Houghton Mifflin Company, Boston, MA.

City Council of Boston
1895   *Reports of the Proceedings of the City Council of Boston for the Year Commencing Monday, January 1, 1894, and Ending Saturday, January 5, 1895*. Rockwell and Churchill, City Printers, Boston, MA.

City of Boston (COB)
1890   *A Report of the Record Commissioners of the City of Boston, Containing Dorchester Births, Marriages, and Deaths, to the End of 1825*. City of Boston, MA.
1899   "Boston Marriages 1741–1751." In "Document 150 Boston Marriages 1700–1751,"
in *Documents of the City of Boston for the Year 1898 in Three Volumes*, vol. 3. Municipal Printing Office, Boston, MA.
1910   *A Record of the Streets, Alleys, Places, Etc. in the City of Boston*. City of Boston Printing Department, Boston, MA.

Clapp, Ebenezer
1876   *The Clapp Memorial, Record of the Clapp Family in America, Containing Sketches of the Original Six Emigrants, and a Genealogy of Their Descendents Bearing the Name: With a Supplement and the Proceedings at Two Family Meetings*. David Clapp and Son, Boston, MA.

Cocks, Elijah, and Josiah Cocks
1995   *Who's Who on the Moon: A Biographical Dictionary of Lunar Nomenclature*. Tudor Publishers, Greensboro, NC.

Colby College
2013 [ca.]   "In Their Footsteps, A History of Colby College." Colby College. https://youtu.be/jI8c3NIbR08. Accessed July 30, 2020.

Colonial Society of Massachusetts
1920   "Mr. Albert Matthews Read the Following Note on—Dr. William Lee Perkins (1737–1797)," in *Publications of the Colonial Society of Massachusetts*, vol. 20: *Transactions 1917–1919*, 10–18. Colonial Society of Massachusetts, Boston, MA.

Commonwealth of Massachusetts
1850 (ca.)   "Massachusetts, Compiled Marriages, 1633–1850." https://www.ancestry.com/search/collections/7853/. Accessed July 30, 2020.
1855   "Massachusetts, State Census, 1855." https://www.ancestry.com/search/collections/4472. Accessed July 30, 2020.
1915 (ca.)   "Massachusetts, Marriage Records, 1840–1915." https://www.ancestry.com/search/collections/2511/. Accessed July 30, 2020

Cunningham, Henry Winchester
1901   *Andrew Cunningham of Boston, and Some of His Descendants*. New-England Historic Genealogical Society, Boston, MA.

Cushing, George

    1965 [ca.]   *Exterior View of the Old Corner Bookstore before Restoration, Washington Street and School Street, Boston, Mass., 1960s.* PC001: General Photographic Collection, Historic New England, Boston, MA.

Daniel, Seth

    2017   "Memorial Hall Receives Grant, Efforts Now on to Restore Historic Building." *Patriot Bridge*, January 13.

    2019   "Memorial Hall Project Pegged at $500k." *Patriot Bridge*, February 22.

Detwiller, Frederick C.

    1976   *Paul Revere Association Properties: Architectural-Historical Analysis.* Society for the Preservation of New England Antiquities, Boston, MA.

    1979   *Historic Structures Report, Shirley Eustis House.* Society for the Preservation of New England Antiquities, Boston, MA.

Dorchester Historical Society (DHS)

    1890a [ca.]   *Field House, Fields Corner.* DHS, Boston, MA.

    1890b [ca.]   *Sarah Baker House.* DHS, Boston, MA.

    1890c [ca.]   *Tileston House.* DHS, Boston, MA.

    1957   Untitled image of the Lemuel Clap House move. DHS, Boston, MA.

    1960   *Dorchester Historical Society and Its Three Houses.* Thomas Todd Company, Boston, MA.

Drake, Francis S.

    1905   *The Town of Roxbury, Its Memorable Persons and Places, Its History and Antiques, with Numerous Illustrations of Its Old Landmarks and Noted Personages.* Municipal Printing Office. Boston, MA.

Floyd, Margaret Henderson

    1979   "Measured Drawings of the Hancock House by John Hubbard Sturgis: A Legacy to the Colonial Revival." In *Architecture in Colonial Massachusetts: A Conference Held by the Colonial Society of Massachusetts September 18 and 20, 1974,* 87–111. Colonial Society of Massachusetts, Boston MA.

Foster, Hannah Webster

    1797   *The Coquette, or, The History of Eliza Wharton: A Novel Founded on Fact by a Lady of Massachusetts.* Samuel Etheridge for E. Larkin, Boston, MA.

    1855   *The Coquette, or, The History of Eliza Wharton: A Novel Founded on Fact by a Lady of Massachusetts.* New ed. William P. Etheridge and Company, Boston, MA.

Frothingham, Richard

    1875   *The Centennial: Battle of Bunker Hill.* Little, Brown and Company, Boston, MA.

G. W. Bromley and Co.

    1884   *Atlas of the City of Boston: Dorchester: Volume Three: From Actual Surveys and Official Records.* G. W. Bromley and Co., Philadelphia, PA.

    1889   *Atlas of the City of Boston: From Actual Surveys and Official Records. By Geo. W. Walter S. Bromley. Vol. 5: Dorchester.* G. W. Bromley and Co., Philadelphia, PA.

    1892   *Atlas of the City of Boston: Charlestown.* G. W. Bromley and Co., Philadelphia, PA.

    1894   *Atlas of the City of Boston, Vol. 5, Dorchester, Mass.* G. W. Bromley and Co., Philadelphia, PA.

    1904   *Atlas of the City of Boston, Vol. 5, Dorchester, 4th Ed.* G. W. Bromley and Co., Philadelphia, PA.

    1912   *Atlas of the City of Boston, Charlestown and East Boston.* G. W. Bromley and Co., Philadelphia, PA.

    1918   *Atlas of the City of Boston, Dorchester.* G. W. Bromley and Co., Philadelphia, PA.

Greenwood, F.W.P.

    1833   *A History of King's Chapel, in Boston.* Carter Hendee and Co., Boston, MA.

Guarino, Robert E.

    2011   *Beacon Street: Its Buildings and Residents.* History Press, Charleston, SC.

Halliday, William H.

    1893   *Halliday's Collection of Photographs of Old and Historic Buildings in New England.* Halliday Historic Photograph Co., Boston, MA.

Harris, Edward Doubleday

1885    "The New England Royalls." In *The New England Historical and Genealogical Register*, 39: 348–58. New England Historic Genealogical Society, Boston, MA.

Haskell, Arthur

1934    *Historic American Buildings Survey, Arthur C. Haskell, Photographer September, 1934 (b) Int- Northwest Room, Second Floor - Marshall-Hancock House, 10 Marshall Street, Boston, Suffolk County, MA.* HABS MASS, 13-BOST,41A, Historic American Buildings Survey, Arts and Photographs Division, Library of Congress, Washington, DC.

Hassam, John Tyler

1884    "Ezekiel Cheever and Some of His Descendants." In *The New England Historical and Genealogical Register*, 38: 170–93. Press of David Clapp and Son, Boston, MA.

Hawes, Josiah J.

1865    *Old Corner Bookstore Washington and School Sts.* Boston Public Library Print Department, Boston, MA.

Heitert, Kristen, Nichole A. Gillis, Kate Erickson, and Heather Olson

2014    "Archaeological Site Examination and Archaeological Monitoring and Documentation, Paul Revere House Education Center Project." Public Archaeology Laboratory, Inc. On file at the Massachusetts Historical Commission, Boston, MA.

Hill, Hamilton Andrews

1890    *History of the Old South Church (Third Church) Boston: 1669–1884.* Vol. 1. Houghton, Mifflin and Company, Boston, MA.

Hill, Samuel

1789    *View of Faneuil-Hall in Boston, Massachusetts.* Illustration in AP2.A2 M4, General Collections, Library of Congress. Washington, DC.

Historic Boston, Incorporated (HBI)

2010 (ca.)    "Spooner Lambert House." HBI. https://historicboston.org/portfolio_page /spooner-lambert-house/. Accessed May 12, 2020.

2011    "Getting to the Heart of the Matter in Fields Corner. . . ." HBI. https://historicboston. org/getting-to-the-heart-of-the-matter-in-fields-corner/. December 22.

2015a    "Fowler Clark Epstein Farm." HBI. https://historicboston.org/portfolio_page/ fowler-clark-epstein-farm/. Accessed April 28, 2020.

2015b    "Fowler Clark Epstein Farm" (Image). HBI.

2017 (ca.)    "Hurd House." HBI. https:// historicboston.org/portfolio_page/hurd-house/. Accessed May 20, 2020.

Historic New England (HNE)

1865 [ca.]    *Exterior View of the Shirley-Eustis House, Roxbury, Mass.* PC001.02.01. USMA.2540.0530.001: Historic New England, Boston, MA.

1934    *Greetings from the Oldest House on Beacon Hill.* PC001.02.01.USMA.0340.6410.002: Historic New England, Boston, MA.

Historic Preservation and Design

2007    "Blake House 2007 Wall Report." Historic Preservation and Design, Salem, MA.

History Project

1999    *Improper Bostonians: Lesbian and Gay History from the Puritans to Playland.* Beacon Hill Press, Boston, MA.

Holden, Edward Singleton

1897    *Memorials of William Cranch Bond: Director of the Harvard College Observatory, 1840–1859, and of His Son George Phillips Bond, Director of the Harvard College Observatory, 1859–1865.* C. A. Murdock and Company, San Francisco, CA.

Hopkins, Griffith M.

1874    *Atlas of the County of Suffolk, Massachusetts: Vol. 3rd, Including Boston and Dorchester: From Actual Surveys and Official Records.* Norman B. Leventhal Map Center, Boston Public Library, Boston, MA.

Jackson, Robert Tracy

1907    "History of the Oliver, Vassall and Royall

Houses in Dorchester, Cambridge and Medford." *Genealogical Magazine* 2, no. 1.

Jenks, Henry F.

1886    *Catalogue of the Boston Public Latin School, Established in 1635: With an Historical Sketch.* Boston Latin School Association, Boston, MA.

Kueny, Nancy Hayford

2019    "Historic Houses of the Month: The Gambrel Houses." *Charlestown Patriot-Bridge,* December 13.

Lanning, Michael Lee.

2005    *African Americans in the Revolutionary War.* Citadel Press, New York, NY.

Leach, John

1780    *Plan of the New Streets of Charlestown with the Alterations of the Old.* Maps1 Massachusetts 1887 001. American Antiquarian Society, Worcester, MA.

Library of Congress (LOC)

1900 [ca,]    *Old Corner Bookstore, First Brick Building in Boston.* Detroit Publishing Company photograph collection, Prints and Photographs Division, LOC, Washington, DC.

1937    *Roger Clap House, 199 Boston Street (Moved from 25 Willow Court), Dorchester, Suffolk County, MA.* HABS MASS,13-DORCH,2-, Historic American Buildings Survey, Prints and Photographs Division, LOC, Washington, DC.

1941a    *Clough-Langdon House, 21 Unity Street, Boston, Suffolk County, MA.* HABS MASS, 13-BOST,8-, Historic American Buildings Survey, Prints and Photographs Division, LOC, Washington, DC.

1941b    *Historic American Buildings Survey Frank O. Branzetti, Photographer Feb. 11, 1941 (a) EXT.—FRONT, LOOKING NORTH— Moses Pierce House, 29 North Square, Boston, Suffolk County, MA.* HABS MASS, 13-BOST,57—1, Historic American Buildings Survey, Prints and Photographs Division, LOC, Washington, DC.

1999    "Allen and Ticknor." LC Name Authority File. http://id.loc.gov/authorities/names /n85316842.html. Accessed June 22, 2020.

Linsdell, Robert

2013a    *Boston Light, Little Brewster Island, Boston.* https://commons.wikimedia.org/wiki /File:Boston_Light,_Little_Brewster_Island, _Boston_(493436)_(10773091353).jpg. Accessed May 12, 2020.

2013b    *Boston Light, Little Brewster Island, Boston.* https://commons.wikimedia.org /wiki/File:Boston_Light,_Little_Brewster _Island,_Boston_(493416)_(10772877893) .jpg. Accessed May 12, 2020.

Mallory, Richard P., and James Millie

1848    *Panoramic View from Bunker Hill Monument.* Norman B. Leventhal Map Center, Boston Public Library, Boston, MA.

Marchione, William P.

1998–2001    "Hannah Foster: Brighton's Pioneer Novelist." Brighton Allston Historical Society. http://www.bahistory.org/HistoryFoster.html. Accessed May 12, 2020.

Massachusetts Historical Commission (MHC)

1973    "Dillaway-Thomas House," Historic Resources Inventory Form B. Massachusetts Cultural Resources Information System (MACRIS) Online Database. http://mhc -macris.net/Details.aspx?MhcId=BOS.11337. Accessed December 18, 2015.

1978a    "Daniels, Richard—Goldsmith, Henry L. House," Historic Resources Inventory Form B. MACRIS Online Database. http://mhc -macris.net/Detailsaspx?MhcId=BOS.10665. Accessed December 18, 2015.

1978b    "Gardner, Col. Thomas House," Historic Resources Inventory Form B. MACRIS Online Database. http://mhc -macris.net/Details.aspx?MhcId=BOS.8230. Accessed December 18, 2015.

1978c    "Smith, Ebenezer House," Historic Resources Inventory Form B. MACRIS Online Database. http://mhc-macris.net

/Details.aspx?MhcId=BOS.8295. Accessed December 18, 2015.

1980a "Cunningham, Andrew House," Historic Resources Inventory Form B. MACRIS Online Database. http://mhc-macris.net/Details.aspx?MhcId=BOS.2126. Accessed December 18, 2015.

1980b "Old South Building," Historic Resources Inventory Form B. MACRIS Online Database. http://mhc-macris.net/Details.aspx?MhcId=-BOS.2112. Accessed April 27, 2020.

1980c "Old South Meeting House," Historic Resources Inventory Form B. MACRIS Online Database. http://mhc-macris.net/Details.aspx?MhcId=BOS.2113. Accessed December 18, 2015.

1981 "Boston Light Station Tower and Entryway," Historic Resources Inventory Form B. MACRIS Online Database. http://mhc-macris.net/Details.aspx?MhcId=BOS.9267. Accessed April 24, 2020.

1983 "Troutbeck, Rev. John House–Linden Hall," Historic Resources Inventory Form B. MACRIS Online Database. http://mhc-macris.net/Details.aspx?MhcId=BOS.8997. Accessed December 18, 2015.

1986 "Thompson, Timothy House," Historic Resources Inventory Form B. MACRIS Online Database. http://mhc-macris.net/Details.aspx?MhcId=BOS.4633. Accessed April 29, 2020.

1987a "Newhall, Henry—Ward, William Buidling [sic]," Historic Resources Inventory Form B. MACRIS Online Database. http://mhc-macris.net/Details.aspx?MhcId=BOS.5349. Accessed April 27, 2020.

1987b (ca.) "Revere, Paul House," Historic Resources Inventory Form B. MACRIS Online Database. http://mhc-macris.net/Details.aspx?MhcId=BOS.5388. Accessed December 18, 2015.

1987c "Warren Tavern," Historic Resources Inventory Form B. MACRIS Online Database. http://mhc-macris.net/Details.aspx?MhcId=BOS.4628, Accessed December 18, 2015.

1987d "Wiley, William House," Historic Resources Inventory Form B. MACRIS Online Database. http://mhc-macris.net/Details.aspx?MhcId=BOS.5011. Accessed April 29, 2020.

1988 (ca.) "Salem Turnpike Hotel," Historic Resources Inventory Form B. MACRIS Online Database. http://mhc-macris.net/Details.aspx?MhcId=BOS.4421. Accessed April 29, 2020.

1989a "Hancock, Ebenezer House—Marshall House," Historic Resources Inventory Form B. MACRIS Online Database. http://mhc-macris.net/Details.aspx?MhcId=BOS.1862. Accessed December 18, 2015.

1989b "Pierce, Moses—Hichborn, Nathaniel House," Historic Resources Inventory Form B. MACRIS Online Database. http://mhc-macris.net/Details.aspx?MhcId=BOS.5389. Accessed December 18, 2015.

1990 "Clough, Ebenezer House," Historic Resources Inventory Form B. MACRIS Online Database. http://mhc-macris.net/Details.aspx?MhcId=BOS.5487. Accessed June 20, 2020.

1995 "Field's Corner," Historic Resources Inventory Form A. MACRIS Online Database. http://mhc-macris.net/details.aspx?mhcid=BOS.DQ. Accessed April 28, 2020.

1999 "Loring-Greenough House," Historic Resources Inventory Form B. MACRIS Online Database. http://mhc-macris.net/Details.aspx?MhcId=BOS.10164. Accessed December 18, 2015.

2000 "Old Corner Bookstore," Historic Resources Inventory Form B. MACRIS Online Database. http://mhc-macris.net/Details.aspx?MhcId=BOS.2127. Accessed December 18, 2015.

2007a "Blake, James House," Historic Resources Inventory Form B. MACRIS Online Database. http://mhc-macris.net/Details.aspx?MhcId=BOS.5804. Accessed December 18, 2015.

2007b "King's Chapel," Historic Resources Inventory Form B. MACRIS Online Database.

http://mhc-macris.net/Details.aspx?MhcId=BOS.2067. Accessed December 18, 2015.

2007c  "Old State House," Historic Resources Inventory Form B. MACRIS Online Database. http://mhc-macris.net/Details.aspx?MhcId=BOS.2107. Accessed December 18, 2015.

2007d  "Union Oyster House," Historic Resources Inventory Form B. MACRIS Online Database. http://mhc-macris.net/Details.aspx?MhcId=BOS.2101. Accessed December 18, 2015.

Massachusetts Vital Records

1915 (ca.)  *Massachusetts Vital Records, 1840–1911.* New England Historic Genealogical Society. Boston, MA.

McGlenen, Edward W.

1899  "Landmarks." In *The Dorchester Book*, 51–55. Branch Alliance of Christ Church (Unitarian), Dorchester. Boston, MA.

McNamee, Stephen J.

2013  *Inheritance and Wealth in America.* Springer Science and Business Media, New York.

McRae, Wendell

1927 [ca.]  *JPTC ladies, late 1920s.* Jamaica Plain Tuesday Club Records, Jamaica Plain, MA.

Middlesex County

Multiple years  *Middlesex County Massachusetts Probate Records* (MCMPR). Middlesex County, MA. "Probate Records 1648–1924 (Middlesex County, Massachusetts)." www.familysearch.org.

Multiple years  *Middlesex Registry of Deeds* (MRD). Middlesex County, MA. In "Massachusetts Land Records 1620–1860, Middlesex." www.familysearch.org.

Miles, D W.H., and Michael Worthington

2007  "The Tree-Ring Dating of the Blake House, Dorchester, Suffolk County, Massachusetts." Oxford Dendrochronology Laboratory, Reading, United Kingdom.

Miles, D.W.H., Michael. J. Worthington, and Anne Andrus Grady

2002  "Development of Standard Tree-Ring Chronologies for Dating Historic Structures in Eastern Massachusetts, Phase II, Massachusetts Historical Commission Survey and Planning Grant Completion Report." Oxford Dendrochronology Laboratory, Reading, United Kingdom.

National Archives and Records Administration

1976  "Ezra Badlam," Massachusetts 9th Regiment. In "U.S. Compiled Revolutionary War Military Service Records, 1775–1783." https://www.ancestry.com/search/collections/1309/. Accessed April 28, 2020.

National Park Service (NPS)

1969  "Old North Church," National Register of Historic Places Inventory-Nomination Form. MACRIS Online Database. http://mhc-macris.net/Details.aspx?MhcId=BOS.CV. Accessed December 18, 2015.

1975  "Paul Revere House," National Register of Historic Places Inventory. NPS. MACRIS Online Database. http://mhc-macris.net/details.aspx?mhcid=BOS.5388. Accessed July 30, 2020.

1977  "Shirley-Eustis House," National Register of Historic Places Inventory-Nomination Form. MACRIS Online Database. http://mhc-macris.net/Details.aspx?MhcId=BOS.12785. Accessed December 18, 2015.

1985  "Hurd House," Historic Preservation Certification Application. NPS.

1991  "Long Wharf and Custom House Block," National Register of Historic Places Inventory-Nomination Form. MACRIS Online Database. http://mhc-macris.net/Details.aspx?MhcId=BOS.AQ. Accessed April 28, 2020.

2009  "Pierce House," National Register of Historic Places Inventory. NPS. MACRIS Online Database. http://mhc-macris.net/Details.aspx?MhcId=BOS.6136. Accessed July 30 2020.

Nell, William C.

 1855 *The Colored Patriots of the American Revolution, with Sketches of Several Distinguished Colored Persons: To Which Is Added a Brief Survey of the Condition and Prospects of Colored Americans.* Robert F. Wallcut, Boston, MA.

New England Historical and Geneaological Society

 1906 *The New England Historical and Geneaological* [*sic*] *Register. Volume LX: Memoirs.* The New England Historical and Geneaological Society, Boston, MA.

Norfolk County

 Multiple years *Norfolk County Massachusetts Probate Records* (NCMPR). Norfolk County, MA. "Probate Docket Books, and Record Books (1793–1916) [Norfolk County, Massachusetts]." www.familysearch.org.

 Multiple years *Norfolk Registry of Deeds* (NRD). Norfolk County, MA. In "Massachusetts Land Records 1620–1860, Norfolk." www.familysearch.org.

Nylander, Richard C., Elizabeth Redmond, and Penny J. Sander

 1986 *Wallpaper in New England.* Society for the Preservation of New England Antiquities, Boston, MA.

O. H. Bailey and Co.

 1890a *Mattapan, Massachusetts: 1890.* O. H. Bailey and Co., Boston, MA.

 1890b *Milton, Lower Mills, Massachusetts: 1890.* O. H. Bailey and Co., Boston, MA.

 1891 *Jamaica Plain, Massachusetts: Ward 23, City of Boston, 1891.* O. H. Bailey and Co., Boston, MA.

Orcutt, William Dana

 1893 *Good Old Dorchester: A Narrative History of the Town, 1630–1893.* William Dana Orcutt, Boston, MA.

Osgood, James R.

 1873 *Old Landmarks and Historic Personages of Boston.* James R. Osgood and Company, Boston, MA.

"Paul Revere."

 1730 *Weekly News-Letter,* no. 177. May 21.

Paul Revere Memorial Association

 2019 *Courtyard of the Paul Revere House.* Paul Revere Memorial Association, Boston, MA.

Penniman, John R.

 1799 *Meetinghouse Hill, Roxbury, Massachusetts.* Centennial Year Acquisition and Centennial Year Major Acquisition funds, 1979.1461, Art Institute of Chicago, Chicago, IL.

Pierrie, William, and James Newton

 1776 *A View of Boston Taken on the Road to Dorchester.* Norman B. Leventhal Map Center Collection, Boston, MA.

Poulsen, Jennifer

 2011 "Urban Consumption in Late 19th-Century Dorchester." MA thesis, University of Massachusetts Boston.

Price, William, and John Bonner

 1769 *A New Plan of ye Great Town of Boston in New England in America, with the Many Additionall* [*sic*] *Buildings, & New Streets, to the Year, 1769.* Norman B. Leventhal Map Center Collection, Boston, MA.

"Restoration of the Paul Revere House, Boston."

 1914 *Architectural Record* 36, 80.

Revere, Paul

 1768 *A View of Part of the Town of Boston in New-England and Brittish* [*sic*] *Ships of War Landing their Troops! 1768.* Norman B. Leventhal Map Center Collection, Boston, MA.

 1770 *The Bloody Massacre Perpetrated in King Street Boston on March 5th 1770 by a Party of the 29th Regt.* Prints and Photographs Division, Library of Congress, Washington, DC.

 Richards, L. J.

 1899 *Atlas of Dorchester, West Roxbury and Brighton, City of Boston,* plate 36. J. P. Brown and Co, Boston, MA. Norman B. Leventhal Map Center Collection, Boston Public Library, Boston, MA.

Ritchie, Duncan, and Beth P. Miller

 1994 "Archaeological Investigations of the Prehistoric and Historic Period Components of the Dillaway-Thomas House Site, Roxbury Heritage State Park, Boston, MA." Report on file at the Massachusetts Historical Commission, Boston, MA.

Roper, Stephen J.

1974    *The Early History of the Paul Revere House.* In *Architecture in Colonial Massachusetts: A Conference Held by the Colonial Society of Massachusetts September 18 and 20, 1974,* 3–21. Colonial Society of Massachusetts, Boston MA.

Rugo, Robert

1985 [ca.]    *770 Washington Street.* Photo collection of the owners.

Sammarco, Anthony M.

2017    *Jordan Marsh: New England's Largest Store.* History Press, Charleston, SC.

Sartan, John

1863    *Bostonians! Save the Old John Hancock Mansion.* Thomas O. H. Perry Burnham, Boston, MA. GC002.02.165, Prints and Engravings Collection, 1830s–1920s, Historic New England, Boston, MA.

Sawyer, Timothy Thompson

1902 *Old Charlestown: Historical, Biographical, Reminiscent.* James H. West Company, Boston, MA.

Snowman, Sally R., and James G. Thomson

2016    *Boston Light.* Arcadia Publishing, Charlestown, SC.

Sonrel, Antoine

1870 [ca.]    *Portrait of C. K. Dillaway with Hanafusa Kotarô, Hiraga Isosaburô, Tsuge Zengo, and Aoki Zenpei.* 2002.239, Charles Bain Hoyt Fund, Museum of Fine Arts, Boston.

Stark, James H.

1901    *Stark's Antique Views of Ye Towne of Boston.* James H. Stark, Boston, MA.

Sturgis, John Hubbard

1863 [ca.]    *Measured South Elevation of the John Hancock House.* AR001.USMA.0250.004.001. General Architectural and Cartographic Collection, Historic New England, Boston, MA.

Suffolk County

Multiple years    *Suffolk County Massachusetts Probate Records* (SCMPR). Suffolk County, MA. "Suffolk County (Massachusetts) Probate Records, 1636–1899." www.familysearch.org.

Multiple years    *Suffolk Registry of Deeds* (SRD). Suffolk County, MA. In "Massachusetts Land Records 1620–1860, Suffolk." www.familysearch.org.

Todd, T. J.

2020    "Who Built Old North?" https://oldnorth .com/2020/05/14/99-sure-ep-3-who-built-old -north/. May 14.

United States Census Bureau

1790    *United States Federal Census, Massachusetts, Suffolk, Boston.* US Department of the Interior, Washington, DC. https://www.ancestry.com/search /collections/5058/. Accessed July 30, 2020.

1800    *United States Federal Census, Massachusetts, Norfolk, Dorchester.* US Department of the Interior, Washington, DC. https://www.ancestry.com/search /collections/7590/. Accessed July 30, 2020.

1820    *United States Federal Census, Massachusetts, Suffolk, Boston.* US Department of the Interior, Washington, DC. https://www.ancestry.com/search /collections/7734/ Accessed August 12, 2020.

1860    *United States Federal Census, Massachusetts, Suffolk, Charlestown.* US Department of the Interior, Washington, DC. https://www.ancestry.com/search /collections/7667/. Accessed July 30, 2020.

1883    *1880 Census. Volume 1: Statistics of the Population of the United States.* US Department of the Interior, Washington, DC. https://www .census.gov/library/publications/1883/dec /vol-01-population.html. Accessed August 14, 2020.

1900    *United States Federal Census, Massachusetts, Suffolk.* US Department of the Interior, Washington, DC. https://

www.ancestry.com/search/collections/7602.
Accessed August 14, 2020.

WBUR

2012    "After Century of Silence, Old South Bell
        Rings." *Radio Boston*. https://www.wbur.org
        /radioboston/2012/01/12/meeting-house
        -belfry. January 12.

Webster, Andrew J.

2016    "Ceramic Consumption in a Boston
        Immigrant Tenement." MA thesis, University
        of Massachusetts Boston.

Webster, Margaret M.

1937    *General Plan, Loring-Greenough Place, 12
        South Street, Jamaica Plain, Suffolk County, MA.*
        HABS MASS,13-JAMP,1--, Historic American
        Buildings Survey, Prints and Photographs Di-
        vision, Library of Congress. Washington, DC.

Whittier, Charles Collyer

1907    *Genealogy of the Stimpson Family of
        Charlestown, Mass., and Allied Lines.* D. Clapp
        and Son, Boston, MA.

Winship, John Perkins Cushing

1902    *Historical Brighton: An Illustrated History
        of Brighton and Its Citizens.* George. A Warren,
        Boston, MA.

Wright, Albert J.

1871    *Thirteenth Annual Report of the Board
        of State Charities of Massachusetts: To Which
        Is Added Reports from Its Departments.*
        Vol. 7. Wright and Potter, State Printers,
        Boston, MA.

Yale University

2010 [ca.]    *Chest-on-Chest.* Yale University Art
              Gallery, Yale University, New Haven, CT.

Zimmer, Edward

1974    "The James Blake House: A Documentary
        Study." In *Architecture in Colonial
        Massachusetts: A Conference Held by the
        Colonial Society of Massachusetts September
        18 and 20, 1974*, 61–74. Colonial Society of
        Massachusetts, Boston MA.

# Index

Page numbers in **boldface** refer to main entries of the fifty oldest buildings; those in *italics* refer to illustrations and captions.

Ashmont Hill (Dorchester), late Victorian
neighborhood of, 116
Ashmont Street (Dorchester), 116
astronomy, astronomers, 147
*Atlantic Monthly*, 53
attics, 15, 43, 135
Atwood and Bacon Oyster House, 43
Austin, Margaret Rand, 173
Austin, Nathaniel, 173
awnings, 41, 43, 75

Babcock, Tristan, 133
Back Bay, 3, 4, 5, 57, 67, 79; fishweirs in, 182, 182
Back Lane (Charlestown), 167
Badlam, Ezra, 110–11, 141
Badlam, Hannah, 111
Badlam, Patience Capen, 110, 111
Badlam, Stephen, 110, 111
Baker, Edmund, Jr., 141
Baker, Edmund, Sr., 141
Baker, Patience, 135
Baker, Samuel, 135
Baker, Walter, 141
Baker House (Dorchester), 127
balconies, 35, 37
balustrades, 85, 125
bankers, 168
Barbados, 18
Barker, Lucy Loring, 167
Barnard Capen House (ca. 1637), as honorable
mention, 183, 183
Barricado, 102
Bartlett Street (Roxbury), Spooner-Lambert House
on, 124
basements, 19, 70, 77
Battle of Bunker Hill (1775), 81, 87, 122, 123, 167;
burning of Charlestown and, 157, 158, 173
Battle of Lexington and Concord, 167
bay windows, 47, 82
Beacon Hill, 35; Blacks and, 131–32; Glapion-
Middleton House in, 130, 131, 131, 132; historic
preservation in, 1–2, 4, 5
Beacon Island. *See* Little Brewster Island

Beal, Jacob, 147, 150; house of, 11, 149, **149–50**, 150
Beal family, 150
bells, 66–67
Belmont, 138
belt courses, 29, 43, 52, 63, 66, 107; on Grant House,
70, 70; on Kimball-Cheever House, 50, 50
Benjamin Faneuil Gatekeeper House (ca. 1761),
73, 97, **97–100**, 98, 99; changes to, 100; location
of, 10, 97
Bethune, George, 100
Bethune, Mary Faneuil, 99, 100
Bicknell House (ca. 1785), 127, **127–29**, 128; location
of, 11; moving of, 128, 128
Big Dig, 162
Bird, Abigail, 147
Bird, Calvin, house of, 11, 151, **151–53**, 152
Bird, Charles, 152
Bird, Joseph, 152
Bird, Mary Homer, 152
Bird, Nancy, 152
Bird, Thomas, 152
Bird family, 152
Black Heritage Trail, 133
Blacks: in American Revolution, 131; in Beacon Hill,
131–32. *See also* African Americans; Africans;
enslaved peoples
Blackstone Block (Downtown), 44, 108
Blake, Elizabeth Clap, 14
Blake, James, 14
Blake House (1661), **13–16**, 13, 14; Dorchester
Historical Society and, 27; location of, 11, 15;
moving of, 128; restoration of, 20
BLC. See Boston Landmarks Commission
boardinghouses, 19, 87
*Boarding School, The; or, Lessons of a Preceptress to
Her Pupils* (Foster, 1798), 144
Boies, James, 138, 139
Boies, John, 139
Bond, George, 148
Bond, Selinda, 147
Bond, William, 147
Bond, William Cranch, 147; house of, 11, **146–48**,
146, 147; instruments by, 148

cladding, 8, 162; asphalt siding, 158; brick, *118*, *120*; marble, 161. *See also* clapboards

Clap, Elizabeth, 14

Clap, Lemuel, 26, 27; house of, *11*, **24–27**

Clap, Roger, 25

Clap, Samuel, Jr., 119

Clap, Samuel, Sr., 119; house of, *11*, **117–20**, *117*, *118*, *120*

clapboards: on Clap-Field House, *118*; on Shirley-Eustis House, 77; on Thomas Gardner House, 82

Clap families, 25, 118, 119, 139

Clapp, Frank Lemuel, 27

Clapp, William, house of, 26, 27

Clapp family, 118, 141

Clap-Field House (ca. 1772), **117–20**, *117*, *118*, *120*; interior of, 120; location of, *11*, 117, 119, 120, *120*; moving of, *118*, 119, 120, *120*

Clark, Henry, 135; farmhouse of, *11*, **134–36**, *134*, *136*

Clark, Mary, 135; farmhouse of, *11*, **134–36**, *134*, *136*

Clarke's Square (North End). *See* North Square

clock, clocks: in Old South Meeting House's spire, 66; on Old State House, 35, 37

closets, 70

Clough, Ebenezer: house of, *11*, **31–33**, *31*, *32*, *33*; as mason, 32, 49, 56; Union Oyster House and, 43

Clough, George, restores Old State House, 37

Clough, John, 32

Clough, Susanna, 32

Clough, Thankful, 32

clubs, 123; women's, 145

Coffin House (Newbury, ca. 1678), 15

Colby, Gardner, 170

Colby, Sarah, 170

Colby College, 170

Colonial Revival style, 37, 44, 66

Colonial Williamsburg, restored by Perry, Shaw, and Hepburn, 37

color: of interiors, 37, 56, 66, 75, 84; of window glass, 16; yellow exteriors, 75, 125

columns, 60, 114, 125

commerce and commercial uses of buildings, 46, 63, 66, 73, 81, 103, 120; Brighton First Parish Church Parsonage and, 145; Deacon John Larkin House

and, 158; Faneuil Hall and, 75; John Hurd House and, 160, 161; Old Corner Bookstore and, 51–54; Old State House and, 35; Paul Revere House and, 19; Timothy Thompson House and, 170; Union Oyster House and, 43; Warren Tavern and, 123

Common Street (Charlestown), 176, *176*, 179; Salem Turnpike Hotel on, 178, 179

Community Preservation Act (2016), 185

Community Preservation Committee (Boston), 165, 185

Concord, British troops march to, 57

condominiums, 126, 142

Congregational churches, 84

Conservation Areas, 5

contemporary taste, in restoration, 37

Cooke Mansion, as stone building, 84

Copp's Hill, 122, 131

*Coquette, The; or, The History of Eliza Wharton* (Foster, 1855), 144, *144*

Cottage Street (Dorchester), 16, 147

courtyards, 20, *20*

Cox, Henry, 141

craftsmen and artisans, 110; bakeries, bakers, 122, 123; cabinetmakers, 110, *111*, 139; carpenters, 70, 167, 173, 176; carriage makers, 111; clockmakers, 147; coopers, 43; distillers, 91; furniture makers, 110–11, 141, 179; glaziers, 9, 26, 29, 32, 63; housewrights, 15, 23, 114, 119, 138; masons and bricklayers, 32, 49, 56; metalworkers, 32, 71, 138, 173, millers and millwrights, 110, 139; milliners and hat stores, 53, 170; painters, 73; papermakers, 138, 139, 141; tailors, 43; tanners, 115

Crease, Thomas, 52

Crease House, 63

Crehore, Charles, 141

Crehore, John Shepherd, 141

Crehore, Lemuel, 141

Crehore, Samuel, 141

Crehore, Thomas, 139

Crittenton Women's Union. *See* EMPATH

crypts, church, 58, 85

Cunha, Alan, 123

Cunha, Ann, 123